In the same series:

(continued on page ii)

MODERN LITERATURE MONOGRAPHS
GENERAL EDITOR: Lina Mainiero

MODERN LITERATURE MONOGRAPHS

In the same series (continued from page i)

GABRIEL GARCÍA MÁRQUEZ

George R. McMurray

FREDERICK UNGAR PUBLISHING CO.
NEW YORK

Copyright © 1977 by Frederick Ungar Publishing Co., Inc.
Printed in the United States of America
Design by Anita Duncan

Library of Congress Cataloging in Publication Data

McMurray, George R   1925-
  Gabriel García Márquez.

  (Modern literature monographs)
  Bibliography: p.
  Includes index.
  1. García Márquez, Gabriel, 1928-   —Criticism
and interpretation.
PQ8180.17.A73Z7   863   76-20409
ISBN 0-8044-2620-1

To my wife

ACKNOWLEDGMENTS

I should like to express my sincere thanks to my wife for the typing of the manuscript and her many suggestions for improvements. I especially want to thank Lina Mainiero of Frederick Ungar Publishing Co. for her encouragement in the preparation of the manuscript.

Contents

Chronology

1928:	Born on March 6 in Aracataca, a small town near the Atlantic coast of Colombia.
1928-1936:	Raised by his maternal grandparents.
1936-1946:	Studies briefly in Barranquilla and completes his *bachillerato* in Zipaquirá, near Bogotá.
1947:	Enters the National University of Colombia in Bogotá to study law.
1947-1952:	Publishes approximately fifteen stories of minor importance in the Bogotá newspaper, *El Espectador*.
1948:	Moves to Cartagena, continues law studies, and initiates a career in journalism.
1950:	Moves to Barranquilla and continues to work as a journalist.
1954:	Moves to Bogotá to become a reporter for *El Espectador*.
1955:	Publishes the short stories, "Monologue of Isabel Watching It Rain in Macondo" and "One Day After Saturday," which wins a prize sponsored by the Association of Artists and Writers of Bogotá. Publishes *Leaf Storm*. Travels to Europe as correspondent for *El Espectador*, which shortly thereafter is shut down by Gustavo Rojas Pinilla, the chief of state.

1956:   Lives in Paris without a job.

1957:   Travels through eastern Europe. Spends two months in London. Goes to Caracas to work as a journalist.

1958:   Marries Mercedes Barcha in Barranquilla. Publishes the novella "No One Writes to the Colonel" in *Mito*, a Colombian journal.

1959:   Heads Cuban news agency Prensa Latina in Bogotá.

1960:   Works for Prensa Latina in Cuba and New York.

1961-1967:   Resides in Mexico and works as a journalist, public-relations agent, and movie script-writer.

1962:   Publishes the short story, "The Sea of Lost Time," in *Revista Mexicana de Literatura*. Publishes *The Evil Hour*, which wins the Esso Literary Prize in Colombia, and *Big Mama's Funeral*, a collection of eight short stories.

1967:   Publishes *One Hundred Years of Solitude*. Establishes permanent residence in Barcelona.

1968:   Publishes *The Novel in Latin America: Dialogue* (in collaboration with Peruvian novelist Mario Vargas Llosa). Publishes the short story, "Blancamán the Good, Vendor of Miracles," in *Revista de la Universidad de México*.

1969:   *One Hundred Years of Solitude* wins Chianchiano Prize in Italy and is named Best Foreign Book in France.

1970:   *One Hundred Years of Solitude* is chosen as one of the twelve best books of the year by American critics. Publishes the short story, "A Very Old Man With Enormous Wings," in *Cuadernos Hispanoamericanos*, a literary journal published in Spain.

1972:   Publishes *The Incredible and Sad Tale of Innocent Eréndira and Her Heartless Grandmother*, a collection of seven short stories. Two pirate editions of collections of his early stories, *Blue-dog Eyes* and *The Black Man Who Made the Angels Wait*, are published in Argentina and Uruguay. (Both editions were printed without the consent of the author who would like to forget he penned these works.) Wins the Rómulo Gallegos Prize in Venezuela and the Books Abroad/Neustadt International Prize for Literature.

1973:   Publishes *When I Was Happy and Undocumented*, a collection of his journalistic articles.

1974:   Founds news magazine, *Alternativa*, in Bogotá.

1975:   Publishes *The Autumn of the Patriarch*. Publishes *All the Short Stories of Gabriel García Márquez* (1947-1972). Leaves Barcelona with the intention of living in Mexico and Colombia.

The quotations from the works of García Márquez that are offered in this study have been translated by me. For the convenience of the reader, all titles are offered in English. Please see bibliography for additional information.—
G.R.M.

Introduction

"*In about the middle of 1967,* the novel *One Hundred Years of Solitude* was published in Buenos Aires, provoking a literary earthquake throughout Latin America." The critics recognized the book as a masterpiece of the art of fiction and the public endorsed this opinion, systematically exhausting new editions, which, at one point, appeared at the astounding rate of one a week. Overnight, García Márquez became almost as famous as a great soccer player or an eminent singer of boleros."[1] The preceding remarks by Mario Vargas Llosa, Peru's best writer of contemporary prose fiction, describe the initial impact Gabriel García Márquez's most famous work had on the Latin American reading public. The novel's success on an even broader international scale has been made apparent by the numerous prizes it has won, the critical acclaim it has elicited throughout the western world, and its many translations, which numbered eighteen within a few months of its initial appearance. Although it has been viewed as a culmination and synthesis of all previous Hispanic literature and a complementary reflection of other western literary traditions, critic Wolfgang A. Luchting's comments express many readers' boundless enthusiasm: "Whatever one reads or hears about it [*One Hundred Years of Solitude*] reveals . . . an underlying helplessness in the face of this intensely

1

alive work, a kind of embarrassed secret admission of critical arms thrown away, and of an at first hesitant, then joyful abandon to the seductive powers of the novel."[2]

One Hundred Years of Solitude also represents the peak of the so-called "boom" in recent Latin American letters, i.e., the explosion of outstanding novels that appeared during the 1960s. Reacting against the traditional realism that dominated the twentieth-century literary scene south of the Rio Grande prior to 1940, this phenomenon can be traced to works by such prominent writers of the 1940s and 1950s as Ernesto Sábato, Adolfo Bioy Casares, and Jorge Luis Borges of Argentina, Juan Carlos Onetti of Uruguay, Miguel Angel Asturias of Guatemala, Juan Rulfo and Agustín Yáñez of Mexico, Manuel Rojas of Chile, and Alejo Carpentier of Cuba. These authors' universal themes and avant-garde techniques have inspired the current generations, whose leading figures include, in addition to García Márquez, Argentina's Julio Cortázar, Mexico's Carlos Fuentes, Chile's José Donoso, and Peru's Mario Vargas Llosa. García Márquez has also acknowledged his admiration for—and possible indebtedness to—a number of European and North American authors, some of whom are Sophocles, Rabelais, Cervantes, Defoe, Proust, Kafka, Woolf, Faulkner, Hemingway, and Camus.

The Colombian's fictional world, however, reflects above all his obsessions with Aracataca, the small town near the Atlantic coast of his native land where he was born in 1928. The oldest of a telegrapher's twelve children, García Márquez spent the first eight years of his life in Aracataca in the large home of his maternal grandparents who had settled in the town during the "War of the Thousand Days," a civil conflict that plagued the country between 1899 and 1902. These formative years were to have a profound influence on him because of the local legends and myths he heard from his grandmother and the strong bonds of friendship that united him with his grandfather. On one occasion, when asked where he got his fluent, rich, and yet precise, translucent style, García Márquez replied, "It's the style of my grandmother."[3] He has described his grandfather, after whom some of his best characters are patterned, as "the most important figure of my life." The old man died when the author was eight years old, and, according to García Márquez, "Nothing interesting has happened to me since."[4]

In 1946, García Márquez finished high school in Zipaquirá, a city near Bogotá, and studied law briefly at the National University of Colombia. He worked as a journalist in the port cities of Cartagena and Barranquilla, where he also penned most of his early short stories. From 1950 until 1952 he wrote a column called "La jirafa" ("The Giraffe") for *El Heraldo* in Barranquilla. These articles, which treat news events with light humor and irony, contain many of the elements found in García Márquez's subsequent fiction. He then moved to Bogotá to become a reporter for *El Espectador*. His success in the field of journalism is perhaps best demonstrated, however, by his "Tale of a Castaway." This is the result of a series of interviews he conducted with a twenty-year-old Colombian sailor who spent ten days adrift in the Caribbean in February 1955 after his ship capsized during a storm. Printed in fourteen installments by *El Espectador*, the dramatic account of the young man's ordeal fascinated readers and increased the newspaper's circulation enormously. However, because the tale revealed some unflattering information about the Colombian navy (the boat that sank was carrying contraband), it provoked a series of reprisals against the newspaper, which led to its being shut down several months later by Gustavo Rojas Pinilla, the chief of state. By this time García Márquez had been sent to Europe as a foreign correspondent. There, finding himself suddenly unemployed, he endured for many months the typical hardships of an ambitious but impoverished young writer. For approximately two years prior to the Cuban Revolution, he wrote for several publications in Caracas.[5] He then joined Prensa Latina, a Cuban news agency, first in Bogotá and eventually in New York City. In 1961 he drifted to Mexico City, where he continued his journalistic career, worked for a public-relations firm, and supplemented his income by writing film scripts.

García Márquez's most significant literary production by this time consisted of four books: the novels *Leaf Storm* (1955) and *The Evil Hour* (1962); a novella entitled *No One Writes to the Colonel* (1961); and a collection of short stories, *Big Mama's Funeral* (1962). In 1965, following several years of frustrating creative sterility, he suddenly felt inspired to relate the entire history of Macondo, the fictitious name he had given to Aracataca. The subsequent eighteen months of feverish endeavor resulted in his previously mentioned masterpiece along with almost instant fame and fortune. Toward the end of 1967, he, his wife, and their two sons established residence in Barcelona. Since that time he has published a collection of short stories entitled *The Incredible and Sad Tale of Innocent Eréndira and Her Heartless Grandmother* (1972) and his most recent novel, *The Autumn of the Patriarch* (1975).

In 1974 García Márquez founded a left-wing weekly news magazine, *Alternativa*, in Bogotá. About this time he also bought a house in Cuernavaca, Mexico and announced his intentions to live there for six months out of each year and to spend the rest of the time in Colombia. He has no immediate plans to write more novels, but rather would like to do some reporting on Latin American politics. Since the military coup against the leftist regime of Chilean President Salvador Allende in September 1973, García Márquez has made numerous statements praising the accomplishments of the deposed leader.[6] He has also declared his fervent hope for the overthrow of President Augusto Pinochet (the right-wing general who led the coup) and "his gang of criminals on the Pentagon's payroll."[7]

A shy man who despises ceremony and abhors speaking in public, García Márquez frequently regales his small circle of intimate friends with tales spawned by his inventive mind. According to Mario Vargas Llosa, "Political or literary opinions, judgments of people, things or countries, projects and ambitions, everything is expressed [by García Márquez] in the form of anecdotes. His intelligence, his culture, and his sensitivity display a curious stamp of the specific, the concrete, the anti-intellectual, and the anti-abstract. Upon contact with this personality, life becomes a cascade of anecdotes."[8]

In one of his interviews García Márquez described how a tale, which he has never published, occurred to him one evening in Barcelona when the lights went out in his home. The repairman called in to correct the situation stated that electricity was like water, that both could be turned on and off by a tap and registered by a meter. In a split second García Márquez envisioned a family with two young boys living on the fifth floor of an apartment house in a large city. The children beg their parents for a rowboat, which they finally receive and keep in their room. One night when their parents are gone, they break an electric light bulb and the light begins to flow out like water from a tap, enabling them to navigate about the apartment in their boat. Eventually they become so absorbed in their game that they allow the light to reach the ceiling and are drowned. García Márquez concludes that, "There's nothing deliberate or predictable in all this, nor do I know when it's going to happen to me. I'm at the mercy of my imagination."[9]

His vocal support of left-wing causes notwithstanding, García Márquez rejects social-protest literature as Manichaean (presented only in terms of black and white or good and evil) and overly restrictive of artistic freedom. For him, the "revolutionary duty of the writer is to write well," and the ideal novel is one that "not only moves its readers by its political and social content but also by its power to penetrate reality; and better yet if it is capable of turning reality around and exposing its other side."[10] At a time of dire predictions about the future of the novel, García Márquez's prodigious imagination, remarkable compositional precision, and wide popularity provide evidence that the genre is still thriving. Although his dramatizations of the sinister forces threatening twentieth-century life imply strong moral indignation, his works are illumined by flashes of irony and the belief that human values are perennial. The amazing totality of his fictional world is also achieved through the contrapuntal juxtaposition of objective reality and poetic fantasy that captures simultaneously the essence of both Latin American and universal man.

1

Early Gropings and Success

Between 1947 and 1952 García Márquez published approximately fifteen short stories of scant literary importance in the Bogotá daily, *El Espectador.* These tales, which the author "would destroy . . . if he could get his hands on them,"[1] are characterized by a preoccupation with death and the depiction of surrealistic nightmares and irrational states of mind that are often made more concrete and rational by realistic, meticulously described settings. Although Kafka is probably the principal literary influence of this period, themes and techniques developed by Faulkner and Hemingway have also left their mark. For example, "Nabo, the Black Man Who Made the Angels Wait" utilizes temporal involutions and shifting points of view to develop a tale of decadence and madness set in a feudal society reminiscent of the deep South, whereas "The Woman Who Arrived at Six O'Clock" bears a vague resemblance to "The Killers" due to its objective, transparent delineation of superficial reality, its naturalistic dialogue occurring in a café, and its oblique allusions to a murder. More typical of the stories in this collection, however, is "Someone Has Disturbed the Roses," narrated by the spirit of a child inhabiting the dilapidated house in which he died forty years previously. Generally speaking, these early tales suffer from an excessive emphasis on technique and a tendency toward diffusiveness and incoherence, perhaps because of García Márquez's attempt to achieve literary sophistication at the expense of genuine creative inspiration.

When García Márquez was approximately fifteen years of age, he accompanied his mother back to the scene of his childhood to sell the family home. What he found on this occasion was not the paradise of affection and security he had so fondly remembered but rather a deserted, impoverished community well on its way to oblivion. Mario Vargas Llosa believes that the disillusion caused by this experience led to the young man's obsession with Aracataca and recreation of its mythical past.[2] This second phase of García Márquez's literary production did not actually begin, however, until 1955 when he published the short story, "Monologue of Isabel Watching It Rain in Macondo," and his first novel, *Leaf Storm*. The former captures the oppressive atmosphere of a torrential tropical storm whose monotonous rhythm gradually engulfs the protagonist, also a leading character in *Leaf Storm*, and blurs her perception of temporal and spatial realities. The repetitious phrasing, metaphoric images, and adroit manipulations of the point of view—from the collective *we* to the personal *I*—serve not only to convey physical disintegration and psychic paralysis, but also to intensify the theme of solitude.

This theme also pervades *Leaf Storm*, which unfolds through a series of monologues by three characters attending a wake in Macondo: Isabel, a rather shy woman of thirty whose husband, Martín, abandoned her nine years ago; her father, a retired colonel and a pillar of probity and strength in the community; and her ten-year-old son.* The deceased is an un-

---

* The novel consists of a brief epigraph, a prologue, and eleven chapters containing a total of twenty-eight

named, reclusive doctor, believed to be of French
origin, who appeared somewhat mysteriously in the
town twenty-five years previously and began to prac-
tice medicine. He lived for eight years in the home of
the colonel and his second wife, Adelaida. Because of
his affair with the colonel's Indian servant, Meme, the
doctor and the girl moved to a house nearby that they
shared until she disappeared from Macondo six years
later. Meanwhile the community had witnessed economic prosperity and depression as a result of the
short-lived "banana boom," which ended during World
War I. Ten years prior to his death, the doctor, whose
patients had abandoned him for the banana company
doctors, incurred the wrath of the townspeople when
he refused to treat a group of wounded men brought
to his door during a bitterly contested election. On
this occasion the local priest, a forceful and highly re-
spected man known as the Pup, protected the doctor
from an angry mob of citizens. They refrained from
violence but condemned him to rot in solitude behind
the door he had refused to open to the men in need of
medical attention.

The plot's mounting tension derives principally
from the colonel's determination to fulfill his promise
to bury the doctor—the latter had saved the colonel's
life three years before when he was on his deathbed—
in the face of strong opposition on the part of the town
citizens who are led by the mayor and the new priest,
Father Angel. The colonel finally receives the burial
authorization after having bribed the mayor, and the
novel ends on a note of dramatic suspension when the
rusty-hinged doors of the doctor's house are forced

---

monologues: twelve by the colonel, ten by Isabel, and six
by the boy. The majority of the chapters have two monologues, but the first has four, the second three, the ninth
one, the tenth three, and the eleventh five.

open and the casket emerges into full view of the hostile community.

The epigraph of *Leaf Storm* consists of a brief passage from Sophocles's *Antigone*, in which Creon, the tyrant of Thebes, orders under penalty of death that the body of his fallen enemy, his nephew Polynices, be left unburied and unmourned. Polynices's sister Antigone defies Creon's decree and buries her brother, an act that leads to the dénouement. The similarities between the ancient tragedy and García Márquez's novel stem from the fact that both the colonel and Antigone place the dictates of their own consciences above the decrees of civil authorities.

The title *Leaf Storm*, we are told in the prologue, refers to the "human and material dregs of other towns"* swept into Macondo during the ephemeral prosperity of the banana boom. This avalanche of undesirable elements turned out to be disastrous for the community, bringing greed, moral corruption, and economic spoliation. Its negative effects on human solidarity, moreover, are described by the colonel as follows:

"Ten years ago, when ruin came down upon us, the collective strength of those who looked for recovery might have been enough for reconstruction. All that was needed was to go out into the fields laid waste by the banana company, clean out the weeds, and start again from scratch. But they'd trained the leaf storm to be impatient, not to believe in either past or future. They'd trained it to believe in the moment and to sate the voracity of its appetite in it. We only needed a short time to realize that the leaf storm had left and that without it reconstruction was impossible. The leaf storm had brought everything and it had taken everything away."

---

* The Spanish title *La hojarasca* has the double meaning of fallen leaves and rubbish.

Although we know from history that the banana company was an American firm, the United States is never mentioned in *Leaf Storm* as it is in *One Hundred Years of Solitude*. Nevertheless, gringo imperialism as well as the negative effects of capitalistic exploitation are clearly implied in both novels.

Far more important than ideologies, however, are the anguished narrators' stylized testimonials of the process of Macondo's decline. *Leaf Storm* may be classified as a stream-of-consciousness novel, but the majority of its monologues resemble soliloquies more than direct interior monologues. The basic difference is that soliloquy reveals a level of consciousness closer to the surface and thus conveys plot and emotions in a more coherent fashion, whereas the direct interior monologue attempts to communicate a deeper psychic reality by probing the prespeech levels of consciousness.

The child's monologues, which frame the novel, serve to delineate setting and create an atmosphere of mystery and ambiguity arising from his ignorance of past events. Isabel's monologues expand the reader's awareness of the doctor's life and foreshadow incidents that are more fully explained by her father. Her recollections of her unsuccessful marriage also reinforce the theme of loneliness set forth in the story of the doctor, whose tormented existence constitutes the principal plot thread. The colonel's monologues not only uncover information about the distant past but also highlight his present conflict with the local authorities and the townspeople who would prevent the doctor's burial in the local cemetery.

The technique of filtering the fictional material through the minds of three passive narrators sharpens the focus and locks them into their respective consciousnesses, thus intensifying the novel's overriding impression of individual isolation. This penetration of

three psychic worlds, replete with temporal dislocations and contrapuntal compositional devices, makes
time a vehicle for the poetic treatment of the two major themes: decadence and solitude.

Like numerous twentieth-century writers, such
as James Joyce and Virginia Woolf, García Márquez
compresses clock time within a limited frame while
exploring the vastly expanded temporal realms of his
characters' minds. In *Leaf Storm* the wake occurs
between two-thirty and three o'clock Wednesday
afternoon, September 12, 1928, but the story's principal actions take place between 1903, when the doctor arrived in Macondo, and the day of his death.
The seemingly haphazard juxtaposition of past events,
generally pinpointed by specific dates, with present
moments, fragments time and renders the illusion of
a prolonged, arrested present, which serves to reflect
Macondo's stagnant atmosphere and convey a pervasive feeling of futility. The impression of stalled
time is also rendered by repetitions on the part of the
three narrators, each of whom, for example, alludes to
the whistle of the two-thirty train, the closing of the
coffin, the mayor's arrival, and numerous snatches of
the same conversations. An antilinear, cubistic technique is utilized, moreover, to depict the doctor, an
enigmatic figure seen only from without, principally
by three different viewers: the colonel, who regards
him with a mixture of pity, sympathy, and affection;
Isabel, who frequently mentions his "lustful dog-eyes;"
and Adelaida, who objects to his presence in her home,
"as if we were feeding the devil."

In chapters 3 and 4, chronological progression is
interrupted and mystery and ambiguity are created
by a montage of unrelated scenes set forth in the following order: a hut behind the church inhabited by
a woman and her child; the doctor's arrival in Macondo; the Pup's arrival later that same day; the doc-

tor's entrance into the colonel's home; the games the boy played with three chums the day before the wake; and the elaborate meal Adelaida prepared in honor of the doctor whom she mistakes for an important official. This zigzagging narrative chain reaches an ironic climax when the doctor asks his elegantly dressed hostess for soup consisting of grass boiled in water, "Ordinary grass, Ma'am. The kind donkeys eat."

Isabel's monologue at the beginning of chapter 5 resembles the typical inchoate, prespeech stream-of-consciousness and perhaps best demonstrates García Márquez's treatment of time as a means of highlighting stagnation, decay, and solitude. Here the random presentation of thoughts and sensual perceptions recalls Virginia Woolf's reference to the myriad impressions constantly bombarding the human consciousness and her belief that the writer's task is "to record the atoms as they fall upon the mind in the order in which they fall." Isabel's allusion to the difference between the rhythms of "inside and outside time" is also reminiscent of Woolf's assertion regarding the "discrepancy between time on the clock and time in the mind."* In the opening lines of this monologue quoted below, chronological time is brought to a standstill and spatialized by sharp metaphoric images projected onto an inner landscape of surrealistic, dreamlike quality, a device designed to reflect, and thus intensify, the physical reality of Macondo.

There's a moment when siesta time runs dry. Even the secret, hidden, minute activity of the insects ceases at that precise instant; the course of nature comes to a halt;

---

* Although García Márquez has expressed great admiration for the English author, *Leaf Storm* is his only novel, with the possible exception of *The Autumn of the Patriarch*, that shows any noticeable similarity to her writings.

creation stumbles on the brink of chaos and women get up, drooling, with the flower of the embroidered pillowcase on their cheeks, suffocated by temperature and rancor; and they think: "It's still Wednesday in Macondo." And then they go back to huddling in the corner, splicing sleep to reality, and they come to an agreement, weaving the whispering as if it were an immense flat surface of thread stitched in common by all the women in town.

The subsequent montage of mental pictures that come into Isabel's mind includes her father dragging his clogs and dipping his head in a washbasin, her ill-at-ease son gazing distractedly about the room, the barber at work in his shop across the street, the elderly widow Rebeca peering out from a nearby house, Father Angel taking a siesta, and the crippled Agueda reciting her rosary. The repeated allusions to its being "Wednesday in Macondo" and the oppressive presence of death serve to sustain an impression of contemplative quiescence. It is broken only when the colonel enters the room after a conversation with the mayor, and the clock, "Dripping with liquid time, with exact and rectified time . . . leans forward and says with ceremonious dignity: 'It's exactly two forty-seven.' "

Decadence and solitude in *Leaf Storm* are attributed at least in part to past events that weigh so heavily on the present that hope and the commitment to action have been replaced by a kind of passive fatalism. On several occasions both the colonel and his daughter express their belief that the course of human destiny is irrevocable and that their acts have been ordained by a higher will against which they could not have rebelled. The weight of the past extending into the present is also expressed by the recurring images of old trunks full of musty possessions, the lingering odor of a jasmine bush planted in memory of Isabel's dead mother but removed long ago, a rickety kitchen chair where the boy imagines he sees a dead man sitting at night, the padlocked room in the colonel's house formerly occupied by the doctor, the boy's striking resemblance to his departed father, and the long-anticipated stench of the doctor's corpse expressing the rancor of the townspeople.

Occasionally episodes are evoked from the past and juxtaposed with lyrical images of the present in order to convey their lingering effects. Such is the case when Isabel recalls Adelaida's bitterness over the doctor's refusal to examine Meme the evening her pregnancy became known and the colonel ordered them out of the house.

"That afternoon, because of the vehemence of her voice, the exaltation of her words, it seemed as if my stepmother [Adelaida] were seeing again what happened on that remote night when the doctor refused to attend Meme. The rosemary bush seemed suffocated by the blinding clarity of September, by the drowsiness of the locusts, by the heavy breathing of the men trying to take down a door in the neighborhood."

Isabel's solitude results at least in part from her marriage to Martín, a shadowy figure of questionable character whose four-button jacket is a symbol of the mask and thus renders him more "abstract." As she recalls, an air of unreality cast a pall over her wedding when she looked at herself in the mirror on the eve of the event and even then felt the disintegration of her private world.

"I looked pale and clean in the mirror, wrapped in that cloud of powdery froth that reminded me of my mother's ghost. I said to myself . . . 'That's me, Isabel. I'm dressed as a bride who's going to be married tomorrow morning.' And I didn't recognize myself; I felt weighted down with the memory of my dead mother. Meme had spoken to me about her . . . a few days before. She told me that after I was born my mother was dressed in her bridal clothes and placed in a coffin. And now, looking at myself in the mirror, I saw my mother's bones covered by the mold of the tomb in a pile of crumpled gauze and compact yellow dust."

After the ceremony, when Martín asks her what she is thinking about, her fleeting impressions underscore her alienation and depression. "I felt something twisting in my heart: the stranger had begun to address me in the familiar form. I looked up toward where December was a gigantic shining ball, a luminous glass month; I said: 'I was thinking that all we need now is for it to start raining.'"

In her final monologue Isabel describes the Indian servants' efforts to force open the doors of the doctor's house, an action that appears to symbolize the release of pent-up accumulations of the past and the prelude to an ominous future. As the light bursts into the room, she becomes aware of an "invisible breath of destruction," which gains momentum through rhythmically patterned visual images and culminates with the threat of an apocalyptic hurricane—"that final wind . . . that will sweep away Macondo . . . and its silent people devastated by memories." This anticipation of impending doom, though tinged with a note of ambiguity, also prevails in the final episode when the casket is carried through the door. Thus, in spite of the fact that the colonel has obtained authorization to bury the doctor and has been assured there will be no trouble, he appears "agitated, his neck swollen and purple like that of a fighting cock." By contrast, the boy's thoughts are directed to the sound of the curlews, which, according to local myth, sing only when they smell death. "Now they'll get the stench. Now all the curlews will start to sing."

As the novel's central figure, the doctor not only generates much of the action, but also illuminates its major themes. Although in the early years of his residence in Macondo he repeatedly tried to overcome his aloofness, he was unable to escape from the memory of his mysterious past "against which any attempt at rectification seemed useless." When his former patients abandoned him to seek medical advice from the banana company physicians, and the townspeople started unfounded rumors about a romance between him and the barber's mad daughter, he withdrew to his room to feed on his bitterness and await death. His physical isolation and decay became strikingly apparent several years later when an anonymous note appeared on his door accusing him of murdering his vanished mistress Meme and burying her in the garden. After the authorities had searched in vain for the missing woman, the Pup and the colonel went to the doctor's house in hope of obtaining a satisfactory explanation for her disappearance. What they found, the colonel recalls, was "the ruins of a man lying in his hammock . . . covered by the coat of dust that blanketed everything in his room . . . I had the impression that if we scratched him with our nails his body would have fallen apart, turning into a pile of human sawdust."

Because the doctor's physical and moral rot and total alienation reflect the sins and weaknesses of Macondo, he emerges as a kind of allegorical figure, a sustained metaphor of the evil afflicting the dying community. Indeed, the colonel links the deceased to the town when, gazing at the coffin, he senses that he has "breathed in the first breath of air that boils up over the dead man, all that bitter matter of fate that destroyed Macondo." The colonel, on the other hand, combines the eternal human values of love, charity, and respect for one's fellow man that appear to be Macondo's only hope for moral regeneration. His concern and genuine affection for the doctor had crystallized one beautiful summer evening when, feeling the presence of a superior being, he asked his solitary friend if he believed in God. The resulting exchange

led to the colonel's discussion of the Pup, who represents the doctor's *Doppelgänger* ("If you had an older
brother, I'm sure he'd be just like the Pup. Physically
of course.") as well as his alter ego. I.e., the Pup is the
embodiment of the love and respect denied to the
doctor by the community.

Within a short time after its publication, *Leaf
Storm* was widely acclaimed as the best Colombian
novel since José Eustasio Rivera's *The Vortex* (1924).
And, surprisingly enough, when asked in a 1971 inter-
view which of his works he preferred, García Márquez
unhesitatingly replied:

"*Leaf Storm*, the first book I ever wrote. I think a lot of
what I've done since then springs from it. It's the most
spontaneous, the one I wrote with most difficulty and with
fewer technical resources. I knew fewer writer's tricks,
fewer nasty tricks at that time. It seems to me a rather
awkward, vulnerable book, but completely spontaneous,
and it has a raw sincerity not to be found in the others.
I know exactly how *Leaf Storm* went straight from my
guts onto the paper. The others also came from my guts
but I had served my apprenticeship . . . I worked on them,
I cooked them, I added salt and pepper."[3]

In addition to the stylistic similarities between
García Márquez's first novel and Virginia Woolf's fiction, thematic and stylistic parallels exist between *Leaf
Storm* and Faulkner's writings, especially the latter's
As I Lay Dying. In both works a corpse is the central
figure that brings the characters together and elicits
monologues from them, both plots focus on problems
involving the interment of the corpse, and both books
depict societies in a state of dissolution. Moreover, the
time shifts in *Leaf Storm*, the symbolic relations between present and past and the occasional use of
winding, complex sentences sprinkled with hypnotic
repetitions, abrupt syntactic twists, and parenthetic
insertions suggest a stylistic affinity between this novel

and Faulkner's fiction. In the following example from *Leaf Storm*, the colonel is recalling the doctor's refusal to treat the wounded men.

And he answered (and still hadn't opened the door), imagined by the crowd to be in the middle of the room, the lamp held high, his hard yellow eyes lighted up: "I've forgotten everything I knew about all that. Take them somewhere else," and he stayed there (because the door was never opened) with the door closed, while men and women of Macondo were dying in front of it.

As García Márquez himself has implied, *Leaf Storm* is not without defects. Critics have assailed its monotony and lack of plausibility caused by the similarity of the three narrative voices, the result being, for example, that the boy tends to express himself in conceptual language beyond the grasp of a ten-year-old. The following case in point is one of several: "My grandfather seems calm, but his calmness is imperfect and desperate. It's not the calmness of the corpse in the coffin, it's the calmness of an impatient man making an effort not to show how he feels. It's a rebellious and anxious calm, the kind my grandfather has, walking back and forth across the room, limping, picking up the clustered objects." This stylistic homogeneity, however, quite possibly derives from the author's intent, not to convey the psychic identity of his characters, but rather to utilize them as mere intermediaries to relate a unified, lyrical account of Macondo's past and present reality.

A more serious defect derives from two of the boy's monologues involving episodes with sexual overtones that seem entirely unrelated to the central plot. Furthermore, the use of language to obtain a certain desired effect occasionally results in over-stylization as, for example, in the passage depicting the doctor's arrival at the colonel's home. Here numerous repetitions within the host's description of the incident create tension and mystery at first but eventually lose their effect as the reader becomes increasingly aware of technique. Generally speaking, however, thematic unity and dramatic interest are sufficiently maintained throughout and reinforced by adroit manipulation of stylistic and structural techniques.

Leaf Storm dramatizes the steady erosion of moral fortitude and human solidarity in the twentieth century. As the sacrificial victim of this collective tragedy, the doctor not only typifies the lonely outsider so common in contemporary literature, but also symbolizes a moribund society of bitter alienated individuals helplessly awaiting their cataclysmic fate. Though firmly anchored on Colombian reality, García Márquez's first book is universalized by its lyrical depiction of existential solitude in a disintegrating world. Its characters, setting, and thematic preoccupations acquire particular significance in retrospect because they constitute the seeds of a fabulous fictional universe destined to fascinate and delight a wide, international reading public a dozen years later.

2

The Threat of "La Violencia"

No One Writes to the Colonel

On April 9, 1948, while García Márquez was studying law at the National University in Bogotá, the assassination of a popular left-wing politician named Jorge Eliécer Gaitán took place, an act that unleashed the *bogotazo*, the bloody uprising that raged for several days within Bogotá. This date also marks the beginning of what has become known as *la violencia*, a brutal civil war between conservatives and liberals that lasted into the 1960s, causing the deaths of several hundred thousand Colombians. Although *la violencia* has been the subject of many works of fiction, no other writer has treated the theme with the subtle artistry displayed by García Márquez in *No One Writes to the Colonel* and *The Evil Hour.**

As critics have pointed out, these two books in some respects constitute a single novel, both having

---

* According to García Márquez, the principal defect of the Colombian novelists of *la violencia* is their propensity to describe the brutalities of the conflict directly instead of the ambiance of terror it produced. He greatly admires Albert Camus's novel, *The Plague*, because Camus concentrates on the reactions of the healthy to the epidemic rather than on the ravages of the disease.

the same anonymous pueblo as their setting and
several of the same characters. While living in Paris
in 1956, García Márquez, wanting to get closer to
contemporary Colombian reality, began to write *The
Evil Hour*. When, however, one of his characters
assumed major importance, he put the manuscript
aside in order to focus his entire attention on this
would-be protagonist. The result was *No One Writes
to the Colonel*, a psychological portrait of an aging,
indigent colonel who waits fifteen years for a pension
check that probably will never come. Because of a
strong sense of pride and dignity, he attempts to
conceal his desperate economic straits and failing
health with a combination of stoic endurance and
gentle humor that contrast strikingly with his asthmatic wife's bitter complaints and more realistic
assessment of their precarious situation. Nine months
before the story begins, the couple's only son, Agustín,
was shot down at the cockfights for distributing
clandestine political literature. The young man's principal legacy is a fighting cock the colonel intends to
train for three months, after which it will surely win
a large sum of money and rescue them from financial
ruin. Meanwhile each Friday he walks to the dock to
meet the mail boat, convinced that his pension check
will arrive that day. As described below, the novel
reaches an ironic climax in its final line.

Included in the array of sharply drawn secondary
figures serving to offset the protagonist are Don
Sabas, an unscrupulous capitalist who has enriched
himself through ruthless political and financial
maneuvers; the town's arbitrary, corrupt mayor; a
good-humored physician and member of the underground resistance; an indolent lawyer engaged by the
colonel to expedite the payment of his pension; Father
Angel, whose moral leadership consists principally of
enforcing movie censorship; and Alvaro, Alfonso, and

Hernán, three tailors involved in undercover political activities.

No One Writes to the Colonel is narrated in lineal form by an objective, omniscient narrator in a pared-to-the-bone, transparent style reminiscent of Hemingway. The action occurs in 1956 (a reference to the Suez crisis indicates the year) between October and December. The setting is an unnamed community probably patterned after the town of Sucre, where García Márquez's parents lived for approximately a decade during the 1930s and 1940s.*

The colonel emerges as a tragicomic figure, a complex composite of pathetic, childlike innocence, heroic idealism and dogged determination to survive. His existence is clouded not only by abject poverty but also by chronic gastritis, which he blames on the October rains, and the omnipresence of death. The opening lines allude to his difficult economic situation by describing his efforts to make coffee with the last spoonful of grains scraped from a rusty can into the pot. Immediately thereafter his attitude of "confident and innocent expectation" and the feeling that "poisonous lilies were taking root in his gut," initiate the numerous clashes destined to occur between his ideal, subjective world and his sordid, objective reality. The underlying atmosphere of stagnation and futility is accentuated, moreover, by the ringing of bells announcing the funeral of a recently deceased musician, the description of the wake, and numerous allusions to death.

García Márquez's subtle treatment of *la violencia* constitutes an additional, though secondary, theme, namely that of political oppression and the tensions it

---

* Generally speaking, *la violencia* was felt less in the coastal region, where Aracataca is located, than in the interior. Sucre is much further inland.

spawns. It should be pointed out that in 1956 Colombia was governed by President Gustavo Rojas Pinilla, in reality a brutal dictator who had deposed his conservative predecessor, Laureano Gómez, in 1953. Although Rojas Pinilla was theoretically a liberal, during *la violencia* political labels lost much of their meaning. Thus, while the underground in *No One Writes to the Colonel* is obviously fighting for a more liberal and just form of government, no direct references are made to party affiliations.

García Márquez purposely shuns the direct description of brutality so typical of much fiction dealing with war and civil strife. Instead he relies on the art of allusion to activate his reader's imagination and in this way heighten the impact of the political drama. Thus, Agustín's murder is merely referred to obliquely in connection with the colonel's desire to keep the fighting cock left to him. Forbidden propaganda is distributed surreptitiously among members of the underground, including the colonel, while they go about their everyday business. One of the characters refers to the musician's demise as "the first death from natural causes we've had in many years." Sabas's exclamation, "I almost forgot we are under martial law," is provoked when the tyrannical mayor reminds the mourners that no procession, not even that of a funeral, is allowed to pass by the police barracks. The colonel sets his clock by the eleven o'clock curfew. Press censorship and the unlikely possibility of elections in the near future are fleeting topics of conversation when the doctor scans the newspapers he receives in the mail. The colonel's visit to the pool hall in search of Alvaro results in his almost being caught red-handed during a police raid with underground communications in his pocket. Father Angel's role as movie censor, though unrelated to politics, is but another example of the oppressive measures imposed on the citizenry.

The colonel bears a certain resemblance to the absurd hero, i.e., the protagonist whose passion for life enables him to struggle unceasingly against overwhelming odds. The absurd hero emerges triumphant from his confrontation with the world because, although he is tormented by the certainty of ultimate defeat in the form of death and nothingness, he comes to realize that his total responsibility and the commitment to the struggle constitute his grandeur. The writers of the absurd frequently mock rational man's obsessive efforts to impose order on chaos by depicting ridiculous situations that negate reason and illuminate the absurdity of the human condition. An example of such a situation in *No One Writes to the Colonel* is the episode depicting the colonel's visit to his lawyer to inform him that he will seek legal advice elsewhere. He finds the lawyer "stretched out lazily in a hammock . . . a monumental black man with nothing but two canines in his upper jaw." His desk is a keyless player piano "with papers stuffed into the compartments where the rolls used to go." Fanning himself in the sweltering heat, the lawyer sits down in a chair "too narrow for his sagging buttocks" while explaining in a pompous, meaningless jargon the ins and outs of administrative procedures. Moments later the colonel adopts "a transcendental attitude" to announce the purpose of his visit, but the solemn moment is interrupted by the abrupt entrance into the office of a mother duck followed by several ducklings. The lawyer then begins to turn his office upside down, getting "down on all fours, huffing and puffing," to locate the mislaid power of attorney authorizing him to act in behalf of the colonel. As for the colonel's proof of claim for his pension, which documented his monumental and laudable task of delivering two trunks of funds to the appropriate revolutionary leaders almost sixty years before, the lawyer believes it has all but disappeared in the "thousands of offices" of a government headed by seven presidents in the past fifteen years, each of which "has changed his cabinet at least ten times, and each minister his staff at least a hundred times."[*]

The colonel's principal weapons against this absurd chaos are a seemingly inexhaustible supply of good humor and hope. For example, when Sabas complains about his diabetes, distastefully displaying a pill he will use to sweeten his coffee ("It's sugar, but without sugar"), the colonel's analogy softens the sting of his friend's bitterness by injecting a note of irony into the conversation ("It's something like ringing but without bells"). When the colonel's wife, "dressed very strangely, in her husband's old shoes and oil cloth apron and a rag tied around her head," chides him for his utter lack of business sense, he interrupts her, saying, "Stay just the way you are. You're identical to the little Quaker Oats man." When she hesitates to plant roses because of her fear the pigs will eat them, he replies, "All the better. Pigs fattened on roses ought to taste very good." And when she examines his emaciated body and exclaims in horror, "You're nothing but skin and bones," he attempts to belittle her concern by declaring, "I'm taking care of myself so I can sell myself. I've already been hired by a clarinet factory."

The colonel's long-awaited letter concerning his pension emerges as a symbol of ritualistically re-

---

[*] This description of political instability is an example of the hyperbole so characteristic of García Márquez's later works. In reality Colombia had five presidents between 1941 and 1956.

newed hope reflecting his human condition and justi-
fying his platitude, "Life is the best thing that's ever
been invented." This fundamental optimism is re-
affirmed metaphorically when he comes across an
old, moth-eaten umbrella won by his wife in a raffle
many years before. In contrast to her grumbling remark—"Everything's that way. We're rotting alive"—
he opens the umbrella, and, gazing upward through
its network of metal rods, observes, "The only thing
it's good for now is counting the stars."

The fighting cock is the novel's most complex
symbol, perhaps because its meaning evolves, illuminating the existential dilemmas of both the protagonist and his community. At first the bird embodies
hope, leading the colonel to comment, "He's worth
his weight in gold. He'll feed us for three years." And
even when his wife reminds him that one cannot eat
hope, he adamantly clings to his optimistic expectations. "You can't eat it but it sustains you. It's something like my friend Sabas's miraculous pills."

Because the rooster is a legacy of Agustín—
who died a rebel—and because the whole town plans
to bet on it in the forthcoming contest, the colonel
feels an obligation to resist his wife's pleas to sell
it to Don Sabas. Moreover, the longer he keeps it,
the more closely its fate becomes identified with his
own. One Friday the colonel is on his way to meet
the mail boat when he is suddenly reminded that the
trials for the cockfights are to take place that very
day. Hastening to the cockpit just in time to witness
his rooster's successful trial bout, he picks up the
bird whose "warm deep throbbing" makes him realize
"he had never had such an alive thing in his hands
before." As he leaves the arena with it tucked under
his arm, he is greeted by cheers and applause from
the enthusiastic spectators. Though stunned and
embarrassed by the ovation, the colonel feels a cer-

tain pride at the thought that the town has suddenly come to life after having lain "in a kind of stupor, ravaged by ten years of history." When he arrives home, his wife tearfully informs him of how "they" came for the cock during his absence, saying it "didn't belong to us but to the whole town." The colonel's reply—" 'They' did the right thing"—and his firm decision not to sell the rooster, express his solidarity with the community, which he believes has at last been inspired to unite against the forces of oppression. The cock, then, not only symbolizes hope, but ultimately emerges as a symbol of the absurd hero's (the colonel's) fight against fate. And because of the bird's beneficial effect on the townspeople, they too acquire characteristics of the absurd hero.

Immediately after this episode the colonel's cantankerous wife fires a volley of questions at him regarding their desperate economic straits, eliciting his statement that on January 20, the day of the cock-fights, they will have no more worries. Her continued nagging brings the novel to its climactic ending.

"If the rooster wins," the woman said. "But if he loses. It hasn't occurred to you that the rooster might lose."

"He's one rooster that can't lose."

"But suppose he loses."

"There are still forty-four days left to begin to think about that," the colonel said.

The woman lost her patience.

"And meanwhile what do we eat?" she asked, and seized the colonel by the collar of his flannel nightshirt. She shook him hard.

It had taken the colonel seventy-five years—the seventy-five years of his life, minute by minute—to reach this moment. He felt pure, explicit, invincible at the moment when he replied:

"Shit."

Critics are divided on the implications of the colonel's last word, some viewing it as an indication of complete surrender to despair. The word itself unquestionably expresses frustration and anguish. The fact, however, that upon uttering it he feels "pure," "explicit," and "invincible," implies an attitude of defiance. It also suggests that he realizes confrontation with the absurd has given his life new meaning and if victory in this life can be achieved, it will come through commitment to action and revolt, not through passive hope. And inasmuch as he has cast his lot with that of the recently awakened town, his exclamation could be construed as an invitation to collective political and moral action.[1]

The colonel's final reply is also highly ironic because it explodes all previous patterns of his behavior, i.e., his gentle humor, stoic sense of dignity, naïveté, and, above all, his puritanical objection to the use of profanity, as demonstrated by a scene in the tailor shop quoted below:

"Goddamn it, Colonel."

He was startled. "No need to swear," he said.

Alfonso adjusted his eyeglasses on his nose to examine the colonel's shoes.

"It's because of your shoes," he said. "You've got on some goddamn new shoes."

"But you can say that without swearing," the colonel said, and showed the soles of his patent-leather shoes. "These monstrosities are forty years old, and it's the first time they've ever heard anyone swear."

A book of little action and limited plot development, *No One Writes to the Colonel* is saved from monotony by its technical perfection and keen psychological insights. The emphasis on mimetic scene rather than resumé, the rapid, spare dialogues, and the concise descriptions consisting of unique details to suggest a total reality, create dynamic movement and enhance dramatic effect. Reader interest is also sustained by the frequent use of the third-person-reflector technique, which filters the fictional material through the minds of the characters, sharpening the narrative focus and increasing credibility by temporarily eliminating the distant and less convincing omniscient author. Thus in the following example the colonel is seen through the shrewd, morbidly piercing eyes of his wife as he is combing his unruly hair:

"I must look like a parrot," he said.

His wife examined him. She thought he didn't. He didn't look like a parrot. He was a dry man, with solid bones articulated as if with nuts and bolts. Because of the vitality in his eyes, he didn't seem to be preserved in formaldehyde.

Movement is also accelerated and events highlighted by the occasional use of cinemagraphic techniques including the close-up, the speed-up, and the fade-out, as illustrated by the following impressionistic description of the colonel's visit at the home of the dead musician's mother to offer his condolences.* Upon entering the house, the colonel is abruptly confronted with death when he is "pushed through a gallery of perplexed faces to the spot where —deep and wide open—the nostrils of the dead man were found." After having spoken with the grief-stricken mother, he almost loses his balance as he finds himself once again

being pushed against the corpse by a shapeless crowd• which broke out in a quavering outcry . . . He spun his

---

* García Márquez has always been fascinated by the cinema. In 1955 he took a course in film directing at the Experimental Movie Center in Rome. The influence of this medium is most evident on his works prior to *One Hundred Years of Solitude* because of their highly visual quality.

head around and was face to face with the dead man.
But he didn't recognize him because he was stiff and dynamic and seemed as disconcerted as he, wrapped in white
cloths and with his trumpet in his hands. When the colonel
raised his head over the shouts, in search of air, he saw
the closed box bouncing toward the door down a slope of
flowers that disintegrated against the walls. He perspired.
His joints ached. A moment later he knew he was in the
street because the drizzle hurt his eyelids, and someone
seized him by the arm and said:

"Hurry up, friend, I was waiting for you."

The novel's artistic balance is enhanced by its
many contrasts (the colonel's naïveté—his wife's
skepticism; the colonel's strong sense of honor—Don
Sabas's dishonesty; the colonel's idealism—his
wretched material existence; the colonel's dry wit—
the constant menace of tragedy), which create dramatic tension and compositional balance, and its
numerous leit-motifs (the October rains, the tropical
heat, the colonel's gastritis, his wife's asthmatic
wheezing, and the references to death), which generate a lugubrious tonal quality.

No One Writes to the Colonel emerges as a minor
masterpiece for a variety of reasons: its aesthetic perfection, ironic ambiguity, and, perhaps most important of all, the endearing personality of its protagonist, one of the most memorable in Latin-American
letters. The book's intuitive quality and masterful execution can perhaps be explained by the fact that the
protagonist was inspired, at least in part, by García
Márquez's dearly-loved grandfather, and also by the
fact that the manuscript was rewritten as many as ten
times while García Márquez himself was living in
Paris on a shoestring budget. Still, in spite of the un-
favorable conditions under which the novel was written and the dismal lives it depicts, it is far less
pessimistic than *Leaf Storm*, primarily because its

overall vision is directed toward an uncertain future
rather than toward a decadent past. The protagonist's
emergence as an absurd hero, moreover, conveys the
conviction that man's definition and grandeur lie in
the struggle he wages against his adverse reality.

The Evil Hour

Although the setting of *The Evil Hour* is an unnamed community, its plot is based on an incident
that occurred during *la violencia* in the remote town
of Sucre, namely, the mysterious appearance on house
doors of anonymous notes revealing secrets and accusing individuals of all types of misdeeds. These
lampoons led to bitter conflicts, causing many families
to abandon the town. In the first chapter of *The Evil
Hour*, a lampoon found by César Montero on his
front door early one morning accuses his wife of
having an affair with a young clarinet player, Pastor.
Montero goes to Pastor's home and kills the youth
with a shotgun. During the next seventeen days—
the central action occurs between October 4 and
October 21, probably during the 1950s—lampoons
appear with increasing frequency. Eventually the
mayor, who boasts of having pacified the town prior
to the outbreak of the lampoons, is provoked into
taking repressive measures, and at the end of the
novel the suppressed violence bursts forth with
renewed fury.

As suggested by the above summary, *The Evil
Hour* realistically dramatizes the effects of the Colombian civil war on a small town, with special emphasis
on social and moral disintegration. The novel's most
completely drawn figures, the mayor and Father
Angel, embody the corruption, repression, and decadence characterizing the institutions they represent.

The mice trapped in the dilapidated church by Father Angel and his two helpers are symbols of the citizens oppressed by arbitrary authorities. Father Angel's repeated references to having "spent his life imposing morality" on "this exemplary town," where formerly as many as eleven couples cohabited without the sanction of marriage, are paralleled by the mayor's assurances that his regime has put an end to past abuses. ("Now it's different. The new government is preoccupied with the well-being of the citizens.") In reality sexual freedom has merely gone underground, as in the case of Nora de Jacob and her lover Mateo Asís. Movie-goers, fearful of being excommunicated for attending forbidden films, evade the priest's vigilance by entering the theater through a back door. The mayor not only has employed criminals to help him maintain order, but also is enriching himself through bribery and the illegal acquisition of municipal land. The smoldering resentment generated by this oppressive atmosphere is expressed by the lampoons, which consist principally of scandalous gossip directed against upper-class townspeople.

The mayor emerges as a kind of solitary despot as well as the novel's most interesting character. Though never described physically in detail, on one occasion he is referred to as "miniscule and sad" next to the towering César Montero, and on another "he was young, agile and with each step revealed a desire to make his presence felt." He makes his first appearance when, having finally managed to fall asleep after three nights of suffering from a toothache, he is awakened by the shot that kills Pastor and reaches for his revolver. His increasing pain from the abscessed tooth and his oft-repeated, mechanical gesture of clutching his revolver in moments of stress underscore his dehumanizing isolation from the rebellious community the central government sent him to subdue several years before.* His sexual solitude also becomes apparent when the fortune-teller Casandra is summoned to his room, ostensibly to spend the night, and is only asked to tell his fortune. The fact that he is hated by virtually everyone in the community is evinced by the verbal abuse he suffers as he wanders aimlessly from place to place. ("May you have indigestion." "This was a decent town before you came." "Come whenever you want to. Let's see if my wish comes true that you die in my house.")

Still, in spite of his arrogance and corruption, the mayor occasionally elicits the reader's admiration and compassion. Unlike the irresponsible, cowardly Judge Arcadio, who abandons his pregnant mistress and flees the town at the first sign of danger, he repeatedly demonstrates his physical courage, an example being his singlehanded arrest of the heavily armed César Montero in a tense scene reminiscent of a Western movie. His terrible suffering culminates when he and three of his police agents break into the office of the local dentist, one of his most bitter enemies, and compel him to extract the tooth. Instead of describing the details of the operation, which is performed by the vindictive dentist without anesthesia, García Márquez utilizes the roving-camera technique to capture the patient's subsequent reactions, thus making the omitted implicit and even more powerful. "When the most terrible moment of his life had passed, the mayor relaxed the tension of his muscles and remained exhausted in the chair while the dark designs painted by the humidity on the ceiling became fixed in his memory until death."

---

* The political situation in *The Evil Hour* is similar to that depicted in *No One Writes to the Colonel*. The underground is fighting against governmental injustice, but specific party affiliations are never mentioned.

Father Angel also is portrayed unfavorably but not entirely without sympathy. His solitude is accentuated by the precise details of the evening meal he has taken alone in his office for nineteen years, and his extreme poverty by "his cassock with mended edges, his badly worn shoes, and his rough hands with fingernails like singed horns." At first he prefers to ignore the lampoons, considering them a "product of envy" because their targets are members of the town's oligarchy with whom he is allied. His fundamental lack of the qualities essential for spiritual leadership are demonstrated throughout the novel. For example, he is often more interested in trivialities than in truly important matters, a case in point being his insistence that women wear sleeves to confession and his reluctance to come to grips with the crucial problem of the lampoons. His insensitivity and inability to deal with human suffering surface when he passes by Dr. Giraldo's office one afternoon and the doctor asks him if he recalls the pictures taken of prisoners in concentration camps during the war. Father Angel admits that "he didn't remember the pictures but he was sure he had seen them." Then Dr. Giraldo confronts him with one of his patients, an emaciated, incurably ill child, the sight of whom horrifies the priest and precipitates his hasty departure.

In a conversation toward the end of the novel, Dr. Giraldo asks Father Angel if he has ever had misgivings about his lifelong efforts to "stifle human instincts," especially in view of the fact that "everything continues to be the same under the surface." Father Angel's poignant reply—"Every night, all my life, I have had that feeling"—makes him more human as does his secret torment caused by an incident that occurred many years previously. One night he was called to Nora de Jacob's bedside to administer the last rites, and she confessed to him that the father

of her recently born daughter was not her husband.
Father Angel refused to grant her absolution until
she repeated her confession in the presence of her
husband, an act that probably led to the couple's
separation after her unexpected recovery.

The lampoons play a major role in the novel,
representing a symptom of the town's social and
moral deterioration resulting from *la violencia*, and,
ultimately, triggering the renewed outbursts of the
civil war. They exude elements of mystery, partly
because of their unknown origin ("It's the whole
town and it's nobody") and partly because of the terror they arouse ("What keeps people from sleeping
isn't the lampoons but the fear of the lampoons").
These qualities and others discussed below have led
some critics to surmise that the lampoons could represent a metaphor of social protest literature,[2] the type
of fiction that has been so characteristic of Latin-
American letters. This interpretation would seem to
be supported by the fact that the lampoons are
directed only against the rich, the powerful, and the
corrupt. The poor are not only amused by their appearance but experience a kind of collective victory
when the mayor is forced to take repressive measures
and thus, in a sense, retract his boast of having pacified the community. The lampoons' resemblance to
fiction, moreover, is illustrated by Judge Arcadio's
remark, "It's like reading detective novels," and the
diabetic Don Sabas's curiosity, "Be careful, Doctor.
I don't want to die before finding out how this novel
ends." Perhaps the power of protest literature is
alluded to when the dentist, the only rebel remaining
in the town who has openly defied the authorities,
remarks to his terrified wife, "It would be funny if
they ran us out of town with a piece of paper stuck
to our door when they couldn't do it with bullets."

The lampoons provide a major source of thematic

unity in the novel, producing shock waves and triggering chain reactions that make up the majority of
the plot threads. For example, the accusation against
Rebeca de Asís—that her husband is not the father
of her daughter—arouses his insane jealousy and
sparks her mother-in-law's request that Father Angel
condemn the lampoons during Sunday mass. Lacking
the moral courage to take a public stand on the issue,
Father Angel convinces the mayor to intervene, resulting in the declaration of a state of siege and a curfew. The increased police surveillance precipitates
the widow Montiel's decision to sell her property and
leave town. Her actions arouse the greed of Don
Sabas and the mayor, both of whom attempt to take
advantage of the opportunity to gain control of her
enormous wealth. The mayor's zeal in this matter
leads to his unjust arrest of Carmichael, Mrs. Montiel's
administrator, when he refuses to participate in the
official's illegal maneuvers. The pressure to find those
guilty of writing the lampoons also leads to the arrest
and torture of Pepe Amador, whose death brings the
novel to its climax and end.

A superficial reading of *The Evil Hour* creates
the impression of a random-structured work consisting of unrelated scenes whose characters appear and
disappear somewhat haphazardly. Perhaps these very
elements are intended to accentuate the irrational
atmosphere of the chaotic, strife-ridden society depicted. As a defense against this threat of chaos,
however, other aspects of the novel indicate its carefully organized fictional framework. In addition to
its linguistic precision and unities of time and place,
The Evil Hour displays a compositional symmetry of
ten unnumbered units, each containing three or four
brief sections. Moreover, stylistic and structural devices are skillfully manipulated in order to highlight
theme and intensify mood. For example, images such

as the following reinforce the central theme of disintegration by disrupting normal temporal progression and creating an atmosphere of stagnation and putrefaction. "The town was simmering in the broth of the siesta." "This house is burning up." "Although the drizzle persisted, Father Angel went out to take his evening walk . . . he went as far as the flooded sector. He only found the cadaver of a cat floating among the flowers." "The desolate square, the almond trees sleeping in the rain, the town immobile in the inconsolable October dawn . . ." "He lay down to rest in the darkest corner of the room, hardly aware of the intermittent cries of a distant curlew." "Hours later . . . he wondered if time had really passed during the nineteen years he had been in the parish." "The foul odor of rotting flesh remained for a moment over the dock, became mixed with the morning breeze and penetrated to the back part of the houses."

Time is also disrupted and seemingly brought to a standstill by the novel's intricately woven plot threads as well as by the circular structure resulting from the similarity of its opening and closing passages. Even more important is the use of montage, the technique of juxtaposing seemingly unrelated scenes and events, resulting in the spatialization of time and the illusion of simultaneity. This procedure, utilized throughout the novel for a variety of purposes discussed below, is illustrated in the final section of the seventh unit when the actions of several individuals are compressed into a single moment, possibly to foreshadow the anonymity of those responsible for the lampoons. "Father Angel was getting up from the table when the clock began to strike eight . . . the widow Asís heard the second bell . . . The dentist had not finished listening to the news . . . Roberto Asís . . . got up to look at the square . . . Don Moscote was snoring . . . Don Sabas . . . had lost the

sense of time . . ." The section ends with the fortune-
teller Casandra's ambiguous answer to the mayor's
inquiry regarding the identity of the author of the
lampoons, "It's the whole town and it isn't anybody."

Perhaps the most subtle unifying element of *The
Evil Hour* is its tonal quality that serves to generate
dramatic tension, counteract the impression of stagnation and underscore the theme of *la violencia*.
Created principally by the juxtaposition of scenes and
the accumulation of images and events, it also
heightens the impact of individual episodes and creates rhythmic patterns that link dissimilar elements
resulting from the montage structure. Early in the
novel the underlying atmosphere of violence is subtly
suggested when the theater owner visits Father
Angel to discuss his prohibition of movie attendance
that evening and the priest notices that "it was not
a revolver but a flashlight he was wearing in his
belt." Occasionally the deceptively calm surface is
shattered by images expressing the turbulent passions
and senseless brutality that have occurred, and
threaten to recur, in the town. For example, Roberto
Asís's suppressed fury over a lampoon accusing his
wife of infidelity is shown metaphorically when, after
a conversation with her on the subject, he enters the
kitchen and removes the lid of a pot on the stove. "A
turtle was floating on its back in the boiling water.
For the first time he did not shudder at the idea that
the animal had been thrown into the pot alive and
that its heart would continue beating when they
would carry it to the table in pieces."

At times bitter irony is conveyed by the insertion
of passages apparently intended to undermine appearances and subvert meaning. On one such occasion
the mayor tells a group of flood victims they can set-
tle free of charge on municipal land, adding, "We
have to make this a decent town." Immediately there-

after, "A bloody dogfight blocked his way as he turned the corner. He saw a knot of backbones and paws in a whirlwind of howls and then bared teeth and a dog dragging his paw and his tail between his legs. The mayor stepped to one side and continued along the sidewalk toward the police station." The implications of this "dog-eat-dog" scene emerge approximately fifty pages beyond when it is revealed that the mayor has gained title to the municipal land in question and intends to sell it back to the town for a large sum of money so that then it can be given to the settlers and put him in a good light.

The episode dramatizing the murder of Pastor by César Montero creates tensions that reverberate throughout the novel. In this scene García Márquez relies on stylized dialogues and concise, impersonal descriptions of exterior reality to depict characters caught up in a seemingly inexorable chain of events. A wealthy and physically powerful man of bestial nature, Montero awakens in his well-furnished bedroom on a gloomy October morning and prepares for a hunting expedition. While he is putting on his heavy boots and looking for his spurs, the distant sound of Pastor's clarinet is heard playing "I'll Stay in Your Dreams Until Death." The meaningless dialogue between Montero and his sensitive wife, who is totally absorbed in the music, reveals the solitude of each and their lack of communication. " 'It's still raining,' she said . . . 'I feel like a sponge.' . . . 'The tiger gets fat in October,' he said." Tonal intensity mounts steadily with the increasing force of the rain, which strikes Montero's back "like buckshot," and the "overcast sky, two hand-spans above his head," which threatens to engulf him just before he discovers the lampoon on his door. His subsequent behavior resembles that of a mechanically operated puppet, no hint of emotion or purpose being displayed as he directs his horse to Pastor's house, enters the living room, and calls out the young man's name. The ensuing lines sketch Pastor's physical appearance as he comes in from another part of the house, his startled reaction when he sees his armed assailant, Montero's precise movements as he pulls the trigger, and, finally, the strange sight of the dying youth "dragging himself along with worm-like movements over a sprinkling of tiny, blood-soaked feathers."

The preceding episode resembles an absurd tragedy in several respects. Though strongly suspected from the sequence of events, the contents of the lampoon, and thus the precise motive for the crime, are not revealed until later, nor is the fact that Pastor dies in a dovecote next to the living room of his home, the reason for the blood-soaked feathers. The distant, impersonal style tends to ironize events and equate the characters with inanimate objects, in this way underscoring their feelings of alienation and the lack of purpose in their lives. Moreover, like the protagonists of an absurd drama, they are never analyzed or developed logically but merely presented as reacting consciousnesses in given situations. Pastor's murder emerges as an absurd act because the entire episode tends to negate normal cause-and-effect relationships, dehumanizing the participants (the dying Pastor is compared with a worm) and reducing fate, in all outward appearances at least, to pure chance. The defeat of reason is also conveyed by the fact that Pastor's "guilt" is based solely on rumor, a rumor that not only leads to his personal tragedy, but also portends that of the entire community.

The montage of events in the third unit also contributes to dramatic tension by creating rhythmic tonal patterns and accentuating thematic content. Although suffering and conflict characterize each of

the four sections of this unit, as the action progresses
these elements become more pronounced, ultimately
reaching a climax. In the first section, while the flood
victims are moving their meager possessions to higher
ground, the barber speaks sarcastically to Mr. Carmichael about the vast, ill-gotten fortune inherited
by the widow Montiel. In the following section the
mayor's efforts to aid the unfortunate flood victims
are negated by the dogfight, after which he has an
angry confrontation with a woman arrested for allegedly writing the lampoons. Suffering in the third
section is witnessed by Father Angel, who first visits
the dying boy in the doctor's office and then the
mayor tortured by a toothache. The latter's excruci-
ating pain becomes strikingly evident when in desperation he smashes a window with a chair, but the
culminating point in the final section results from
the steadily rising tension produced by the following
events. The mayor seeks relief in a movie, where
the "roaring of warplanes increased the intensity of
his pain." He purchases medicine in the drugstore
but does not dare to take it for fear of being poisoned.
In his room he even seeks relief in prayer. At midnight he hastens to the police station, awakens three
guards and they break into the dentist's home at gun
point. And the cruel scene of the tooth extraction
without anesthesia is followed by the mayor's bitter
accusation against the dentist, ". . . everybody is living in peace and you keep on thinking like a con-
spirator."

In many respects the total structural design of
The Evil Hour resembles that of the third unit, the
inner tensions feeding frustrations, fear, minor outbursts of brutality, and finally leading to the murder
of Pepe Amador. The rising tension level and ultimate
outbreak of open violence can also be traced by a
comparison of the first and last episodes of the novel.

On the first page Father Angel arises, repeats to himself the title of a song played during a serenade the night before, and greets his helper, Trinidad. She shows him the mouse she has caught (a symbol of the long-suffering townspeople) and then informs him of something more interesting than a serenade that occurred while they were sleeping.

"The priest stopped and fixed his silent blue eyes on her. 'What was it?'

'Lampoons,' said Trinidad. And she laughed nervously."

In the final scene, seventeen days later, Father Angel gets up, recalls the same popular tune, and greets Mina, who has temporarily replaced Trinidad. Unlike Trinidad, however, Mina has not caught any mice (the townspeople are rebelling against their oppressors) and the serenade she refers to is not one of music but "of bullets." Indeed, as Mina excitedly tells Father Angel, rumors abound that during the night the police found a cache of arms in the barbershop and that men are going off to the mountains to join guerrilla bands. Her last words, ". . . and in spite of the curfew and all the shooting," are accompanied by her nervous smile, bringing the novel to its end with the implication that the anonymous lampoons are continuing unabated and *la violencia* has begun anew. Another of the final ironies derives from the fact that Father Angel, the town's spiritual leader, has awoken totally unaware of the turn of events because, Pepe Amador's recent murder notwithstanding, "his spirit was at peace" and "he slept like a saint."

The novel's somewhat disjointed, montage structure is also demonstrated by the occasional eruptions of absurd humor and fantasy that clash with the prevailing tragic tone and provide moments of comic relief. An amusing example is an anecdote about old times in the hotel that the mayor evokes while he is

dining in the establishment. "An old traveling salesman used to tell that until the turn of the century
there was a collection of masks hanging in the dining
room and that the guests performed their natural functions in the patio wearing masks, in view of everybody."

Equally ludicrous is the story of the Russian
ballerina who many years previously put on a show
in the cock fighting ring for men only and at the end
of her performance sold everything she was wearing
at a public auction. This episode appears all the
more incongruous because it is narrated by Father
Angel, in the presence of three pious ladies concerned
about the lampoons, in order to demonstrate how
much public morality has improved since his arrival
in the town. An element of black comedy ensues
when one of the ladies recalls a related incident as
it was told to her. "When the ballerina was completely naked, an old man began to shout in the
bleachers, climbed up to the last row of seats, and
urinated on the public. She had been told that the
other men present, following his example, had ended
up by urinating on each other amidst mad shouting."

After conveying his reluctance to speak out
against the lampoons, Father Angel asserts to the
ladies that within a few years he will turn this "exemplary town" over to a younger priest and live out
his remaining days elsewhere. To their expressed
desire that he remain in the community until his
death, he alludes to his successor in Macondo, a
pathetic but preposterous figure symbolizing ecclesiastical decadence. "I don't want to happen to me what
happened to the gentle Antonio Isabel del Santísimo
Sacramento del Altar Castañeda y Montero, who informed the bishop that a rain of dead birds was falling in his parish. The investigator sent by the bishop
found him in the town square playing cops and rob-

bers with the children . . . He was one hundred years old."

Though rare in *The Evil Hour*, flights of fantasy also provide a source of humor. The widow Montiel lives alone in a world inhabited by ghosts, her incipient madness more than likely a product of her isolation and feelings of solitude. At night she wanders through the empty rooms of her large house spraying insecticide and conversing with the former owner, a dead woman called Big Mama, asking her over and over when she is going to die. Her communication with the hereafter is unsuccessful, however, because the answers she receives from Big Mama, "like those of all dead people, were silly and contradictory."

The Evil Hour and *No One Writes to the Colonel* reveal some striking similarities, one of the most obvious of which is their common setting. In addition, several characters from the shorter novel (the mayor, Father Angel, and Don Sabas) reappear and receive more detailed treatment in *The Evil Hour*; both plots occur in relatively short, linear time spans; both works utilize the technique of the neutral, third-person narrator and rely heavily on dialogue; and the style of both novels is precise, succinct, and pictorial.

Unlike its predecessor, however, *The Evil Hour* does not focus on a central figure, but on an entire community, the principal objective being to depict the moral decay of a society caught in the grip of civil strife. Thus, although physical brutality occurs on only three occasions, *la violencia* in *The Evil Hour* is closer to the surface and provides the primary motivation for the action. The humor in the two novels also differs strikingly as illustrated by the colonel's gentle, tongue-in-cheek wit and passages ranging from the ridiculous to the grotesque in *The Evil Hour*. Moreover, in contrast to the perfect unity of action of *No One Writes to the Colonel*, *The Evil Hour* emerges as a purposely jagged montage of juxtaposed scenes spotlighting moments of crisis in numerous lives.

The political issue of *la violencia* remains unobtrusive in both novels, a feature that distinguishes them from traditional social-protest literature and enhances their aesthetic value. In *The Evil Hour* the initial impression of objective realism, rendered by the linguistic transparency and the numerous examples of injustice, is partially undermined by a wide range of stylistic and structural devices. This shift to a more subjective type of art, is also effected by the lampoons, which express elements of the popular imagination, and by the outbursts of humor and flights of fantasy. Thus, by the end of the novel the lampoons have contributed, not only to the subversion of the falsely structured political order, but also to the creation of a transitional form of fictional reality within the framework of García Márquez's total literary work.

The Evil Hour conveys moments of strong dramatic impact, its vigorous rhythms being generated by its purity of style, artistic use of montage, and steadily mounting tension. Its conclusion does not differ greatly from that of *No One Writes to the Colonel*, although the colonel's plucky defiance expresses a faith in the human potential not imparted by the renewal of bitter strife punctuating *The Evil Hour*. Perhaps the most basic difference between the two works is one of tone, the first exuding sympathy, wry humor, and hope, and the second concentrating on man's remarkable capacity for irrational and brutal behavior. Together the two novels constitute a subtly suggestive picture of *la violencia*, a Colombian phenomenon García Márquez has treated with depth, sensitivity, and universality.

3

Big Mama's Funeral:
From Realism to Fantasy

Big Mama's Funeral (1962) contains eight short stories García Márquez wrote between 1955 and 1960. Generally speaking, these tales reveal a traditional Chekhovian approach to the genre, their primary concern being the concise delineation of characters or situations viewed from the perspective of the neutral, omniscient narrator. The setting for five of these stories is an unnamed community referred to as "the town"; the other three take place in Macondo. The action of two is motivated by *la violencia*, Colombia's civil war that began in 1948 and lasted into the 1960s.

García Márquez's favorite story of the collection is "Tuesday Siesta," in which a mother and her twelve-year-old daughter arrive in an unnamed town (more than likely Macondo) after a short trip inland from the coast "through interminable banana plantations" in the third-class section of a train. In the stifling midday heat they walk through the deserted streets to the priest's home, where the woman requests the keys to the cemetery. Her purpose is to lay a bouquet of wilted flowers on the grave of her son, recently shot for attempted robbery. As they are about to leave the parish house, groups of curiosity seekers begin to gather in the street and to watch at the windows. The story ends when the woman and her daughter, ignoring the priest's suggestion that they leave by a back

door, stoically brave the antagonistic stares of the
onlookers and set off for the cemetery.

A classical example of pure pictorial realism, this
story utilizes terse description, scenic action, and
dialogue to capture exterior reality and augment
dramatic tension. The overriding theme is the confrontation between the woman and the priest, the
former emerging as the epitome of dignity and
strength resulting from poverty and suffering (sym-
bolized by the wilting bouquet of flowers she carries), and the latter as a weak, vacillating representa-
tive of an unjust, rigidly structured social system.
While on the train the woman is described as wearing
"severe and poor mourning clothes," riding "with her
spinal column braced firmly against the back of the
seat," and holding "a peeling patent-leather purse in
her lap with both hands." Just before their arrival in
the town, she tells the girl to put on her shoes and
comb her hair. She punctuates her instructions with
"Above all, no crying." When she identifies herself to
the priest (and the reader) as the mother of "the
thief who was killed here last week," he blushes and
asks her if she had ever tried "to get him on the right
track." Her calm reply—"He was a very good
man . . ."—makes the priest realize with "a kind of
pious amazement that they were not about to cry."
And to her comments on her son's physical suffering
while attempting to earn enough money as a boxer to
feed his family, he is only able to murmur, "God's
will is inscrutable," a remark made "without much
conviction, partly because experience had made him
a little skeptical and partly because of the heat." The
priest's general indifference to the mourners is manifested when, anticipating the continuation of his interrupted siesta, he yawns and requests that upon
their return they put the key under the door and, if
possible, leave an offering for the church.

The setting and dénouement of "Tuesday Siesta" strengthen its theme of confrontation, the somnolent town "floating in the heat" and the silent hostility of its citizens suggesting the stagnant status quo, and the woman's determination to leave the parish house by the front door signaling an ambiguous, and thus all the more dramatic, climax. Critics generally concur that this story's precise, evocative treatment of universal tensions make it a masterpiece of short fiction.

"One of These Days" is another fine example of pure realism. The story begins with a brief description of a dentist polishing a set of false teeth early one morning. The mayor of "the town" arrives with an abscessed tooth he wishes to have extracted. When the dentist tells his son to inform the mayor that he is not in, the mayor threatens to kill the dentist if he is not admitted. The dentist's laconic reply, "O.K., tell him to come and shoot me," and his "extremely tranquil movement" as he opens a drawer containing his revolver, set the understated tone characterizing the entire story. Upon examining the mayor's tooth, the dentist states that it will have to be pulled without anesthesia because it is infected. As he performs the brutal operation "without rancor, rather with a bitter tenderness," his remark, "Now you'll pay for our twenty dead men," alludes unmistakably to *la violencia*. In the final lines the mayor's arrogance exacerbates the animosity between the two antagonists, thus leaving the smoldering conflict unresolved and likely to erupt with renewed vigor at any moment in the future.

The mayor stood up, said good-by with a casual military salute, and walked toward the door . . .

"Send the bill," he said.

"To you or the town?"

The mayor did not look at him. He closed the door and said through the screen:

"It's the same damn thing."

Of all García Márquez's stories, "One of These Days" is the most reminiscent of Hemingway's technique. Its terse style, carefully chosen visual details and brief, realistic dialogue leave much to the reader's imagination and in this way heighten the dramatic impact. Thus the fearless dentist is described as "erect and skinny, with a look that rarely corresponded to the situation," whereas the mayor's swollen face and dull eyes reveal "many nights of desperation." The story is framed, moreover, by the images of "two pensive buzzards" the dentist catches sight of while he is polishing the set of false teeth and the "dusty spider web with spider eggs and dead insects" the mayor sees in the "crumbling ceiling" immediately after his tooth is extracted. These symbolic motifs are suggestive of the decadence of a community caught in the grips of social strife.

The protagonist of "Artificial Roses" is a young girl, Mina, who leads a dull, lonely existence fabricating flowers out of crepe paper. In the opening lines she becomes annoyed with her blind grandmother for washing the detachable sleeves she intended to wear to Good Friday mass and, inasmuch as they have not dried, blames the old lady for her failure to receive communion. Gradually the grandmother's intuitive understanding of the girl's enigmatic behavior brings to light her secret disappointment over a broken love affair, the real cause of her pique and, perhaps, her reluctance to attend mass. Meanwhile, Mina's friend Trinidad arrives to help her make flowers, carrying a shoe box with dead mice she has trapped in the church. The story ends with an ironic twist when Mina shrieks an obscenity at her grandmother for guessing her every move and the perceptive old lady exclaims to the girl's mother, "I'm crazy, but apparently you haven't thought of sending me to the insane asylum just so long as I don't start throwing stones."

The protagonist's flowers and the sleeves she must wear to mass would seem to represent the artificial nature of the exterior self she is obliged to display, and the box of dead mice, her shattered emotional existence resulting from the departure of her lover. Though lacking the dramatic impact of the two preceding stories, "Artificial Roses" succeeds in generating tensions by means of symbolic motifs that imply a condemnation of antiquated conventions. The themes of guilt, noncommunication and loneliness are conveyed objectively in precise, linear form, helping to make this story another of García Márquez's most realistic pieces of short fiction.

The longest work in the collection is "There Are No Thieves in This Town." In this tale a good-for-nothing, twenty-year-old youth named Dámaso breaks into the local pool hall and, finding no money in the cash register, steals three billiard balls. The next morning the whole community is agog with the news that Roque, the owner of the establishment, has been robbed not only of three billiard balls but also of two hundred pesos. Because "there are no thieves in this town," a black who happens to be passing through is brutally seized and thrown into jail. Meanwhile, Dámaso and his thirty-seven-year-old wife Ana have buried the balls under the dirt floor of their house, the games of pool have been suspended because Roque is unable to replace the balls, and Dámaso has become increasingly bored with the tedious life in the town. Finally he and his wife decide it would be best to return the loot, and Dámaso once again breaks into the pool hall. This time, however, he is caught

red-handed by Roque, who takes the balls and then
demands his two hundred pesos. When Dámaso denies there was any money in the cash register, Roque's
answer supplies the punch line. "There were two
hundred pesos . . . And now they're going to come
out of your hide, not so much for being a thief as for
being a fool."

The most important facets of this story are its
realistic portraits of antithetical characters and their
dull, backwater existences. Dámaso emerges as an
unstable drifter whose center of gravity is provided
by his stronger, more sensible wife. Thus while he
fabricates impractical schemes for getting rich and
amuses himself at the movies and local dance hall,
Ana concerns herself with the rent, the fate of the
innocent black, and ways of keeping her husband
happy and out of trouble. Dámaso's stupidity is illuminated by the ironic ending when the shrewd,
unscrupulous Roque catches him in the act of atoning
for his crime.

The plot of "There Are No Thieves in This Town"
is based on a well-conceived idea for the revelation
of human weaknesses and the ironies resulting there-
from. Still, in spite of its well-drawn characters and
an occasional vivid scene, the story's artistic merit and
dramatic appeal are greatly reduced by its excessive
length. Indeed, because entire episodes add little or
nothing to the central theme, this is one of the least
successful pieces of the collection.

One of García Márquez's better examples of
short fiction, *Montiel's Widow* is a character sketch
of a lonely and withdrawn woman who is one of the
wealthiest citizens of "the town." The meteoric rise
of her husband, José, to wealth and power by acting
as an informer during *la violencia* is followed several
years later by his demise resulting from a fit of rage.
He was so vehemently hated that almost nobody ex-

pected him to die of natural causes, but his widow considers him a saint and the town ungrateful for its lack of respect for his memory. After the funeral she shuts herself up in her mansion, bites her fingernails, and feeds on her resentment. Her only visitor is the ineffectual administrator of her huge estate, an old black named Mr. Carmichael, and her only contact with the world outside, letters from her three children, now residing in Europe. The townspeople take vengeance on their dead enemy by boycotting his business enterprises and stealing his cattle. The result is that before long his widow faces financial ruin. Unconcerned about her property, she writes to her three children, telling them they are better off in Europe than at home. In the final lines of the story her solitude and preoccupation with death become increasingly apparent.

This tale's remarkably austere and direct style renders an overall impression of realism, but upon closer examination its content appears slightly skewed by infusions of hyperbole, irony and fantasy. In the opening lines José Montiel is described in his casket looking "so well that he had never seemed so alive as at that moment" and "it took clamping the lid on the coffin . . . for the whole town to become convinced that he was not playing dead." Later the reader is asked to believe that "No one in the history of the country had become so rich in so short a time as Montiel."

Mrs. Montiel's naïveté and abysmal ignorance of her husband's evil deeds would also seem to defy reason. Thus while he was "closeted with the mayor in his office for days on end" planning the massacre of the regime's political enemies, his wife sympathized with the oppressed and begged her husband to use his influence to get rid of "that beast" (the mayor). And when Montiel set his own prices for the land and cattle he purchased from rich citizens compelled to leave town, she warned him, "You'll ruin yourself helping them so that they won't die of hunger somewhere else, and they'll never thank you."

Toward the end of the story we are told the widow's daughters send her letters from Paris "written in warm, well-lighted places," indicating their reluctance to return home. "This is civilization . . . There, on the other hand, it's not a good atmosphere for us. It's impossible to live in a country so savage that people are killed for political reasons." One of these letters describes the Parisian butcher shops, where pink pigs decorated with flowers are seen hanging in the doorways. At the end of the letter "a hand different from that of her daughters has added, 'Imagine! They put the biggest and prettiest carnation in the pig's ass.'" Here one detects the mischievous hand of García Márquez injecting an absurd, off-key image alongside a dogmatic political statement, his purpose probably being to blur absolutes through the ironic juxtaposition of incompatibles. This suggestion of absurdity is reinforced by the reference to the "well-lighted place," which recalls Hemingway's famous short story "A Clean, Well-Lighted Place" with its existential message of nothingness in twentieth-century bourgeois life.

The ending of "Montiel's Widow" registers a final note of departure from objective realism. The widow falls asleep while saying her prayers and dreams she sees Big Mama in the patio combing her hair and squashing lice with her thumbnails.

> "She asked her: 'When am I going to die?'
> Big Mama raised her head.
> 'When the tiredness begins in your arm.'"

"Baltazar's Marvelous Afternoon" is a skillfully executed tale of a carpenter whose recently completed bird cage elicits the delight and admiration of almost everybody in "the town." When Dr. Giraldo offers to buy the cage for his invalid wife, Baltazar replies that he has made it for José Montiel's son Pepe and anticipates sixty pesos for his labor. Upon seeing the cage, however, the wealthy Montiel angrily reproaches his son for ordering it without his knowledge and tells the carpenter to take it away at once. The boy reacts by throwing a tearless tantrum, causing the compassionate Baltazar to give him the cage and pretend it was made as a gift. Minutes later in the pool hall, Baltazar informs a crowd of well-wishers he had sold the cage to the Montiels for sixty pesos and orders a round of drinks to celebrate his success. He carouses all night and is seen lying in the street early the following morning.

As the story's central motif, the cage symbolizes artistic creation and illuminates the conflict between the ideal world of fantasy and imagination and that of objective reality. It is described not only as the biggest and the most beautiful cage ever made but also as "a flight of the imagination," "like a small-scale model of a gigantic ice factory, with its enormous wire dome, its three stories inside, its passageways and compartments especially for eating and sleeping, and its swings . . . for the birds' recreation."

Baltazar emerges as the prototype of the creative artist whose child-like nature and sensitivity to the feelings of his fellow men set him apart from the other inhabitants of the town. He wears "the general expression of a frightened boy" and tosses fitfully in his sleep during the two weeks he is immersed in his "creation." Upon realizing the importance the townspeople place on his exacting a large sum from Montiel, he gets "excited" and tells them what they want to hear. That he is basically uninterested in material gain is evidenced by the pity he feels for rich men when he thinks about "their ugly and argumentative wives and their tremendous surgical operations."

In sharp contrast to Baltazar, Montiel is reputed to live in a house where "no one had ever smelled a smell that could not be sold." The two men's antithetical natures also come to light in the episode in which Montiel's son throws a tantrum upon being told that he cannot keep the cage. Montiel advises that they "let him break his head on the floor and then put salt and lemon on it so he can rage to his heart's content," whereas the horrified Baltazar watches the child "as he would have observed the death throes of a rabid animal."

The dichotomy between the realms of creative imagination and sordid, everyday reality are set forth, not only by the two leading characters, but also by the series of events that bring the story to its end. Baltazar has spent so much money buying drinks in the pool hall that he is obliged to leave his watch in pawn with the promise to pay his bill the next day. Later he finds himself sprawled out in the street, aware that his shoes are being removed but unwilling "to abandon the happiest dream of his life." And at dawn a group of ladies passing by on their way to five o'clock mass "did not dare look at him, thinking he was dead."

According to all appearances Baltazar is an unfortunate, defeated human being. He is insulted by Montiel, who calls him an "idiot" and orders him to "get that trinket out of here." Contrary to expectations, he not only receives no compensation for his masterpiece but even spends a great deal of money to celebrate his nonexistent triumph. Ultimately he finds himself inebriated, without the company of his friends, robbed of his shoes and believed dead. Oblivious to his misfortunes, however, Baltazar forges his own version of reality, whether it be a fabulous work of art, his "gift" to the Montiel child, the sixty-peso fee he never receives, or the dream he refuses to abandon. Indeed, in some respects he emerges as the victor. His generosity makes him superior to the avaricious, antipathetic Montiel, and the private ideal realm he has forged in the course of his "marvelous afternoon" casts serious doubts on the worth of his antagonistic milieu. In the reader's mind, the result of this symbolic clash between subjective imagination and objective reality is the denial of absolute values and the ascendancy of paradox and ironic ambiguity.

Although "One Day After Saturday" won a prize sponsored by the Association of Writers and Artists of Bogotá, it is the most baffling piece in the collection. A long, somewhat rambling tale set in Macondo, it portrays three principal characters whose destinies merge in the last paragraphs: an embittered widow named Rebeca; a ninety-four-year-old priest, Father Antonio Isabel del Santísimo Sacramento del Altar Castañeda y Montero; and an unnamed youth from outside Macondo. One day Rebeca notices that the window screens on her house have been torn and, thinking it the work of mischievous children, she complains to the mayor. He informs her that the damage has been done by dying birds, which have been falling on Macondo for several days. Father Antonio Isabel is not as preoccupied with the birds as he is with the devil, whom he swears he has seen on three occasions. Because of his advanced age and weakened mental faculties, he has lost much of his former prestige among his parishioners. He likes "to wander through metaphysical obstacle courses," but he has become "so subtle in his thinking that for at least three years in his meditative moments he was no longer thinking about anything." He is the first person to notice the smell of the dead birds, which he suspects is a trick on the part of the devil to infiltrate the human heart through one of the five senses. He thinks about delivering a sermon on the subject, but his mind is soon distracted by something else.

The priest feels uncomfortable in the presence of the widow Rebeca, partly because she seldom confesses and always replies evasively to his questions about the mysterious death of her husband twenty years ago. One Saturday Father Antonio Isabel finds a dying bird in front of her house and asks her to dip it into water, which she does with obvious indifference to its survival. As he leaves her home, he sees for the first time the rain of dead birds falling on the town and in his mind links the event to the apocalypse. Shortly thereafter, he walks to the railroad station to await the train. There he has a vision of the Wandering Jew, who, according to legend, brought devastation wherever he went and was condemned to roam the world until Christ's second coming, which would occur at the time of the apocalypse.

This same day the anonymous youth arrives in Macondo on his way to an unnamed destination to make arrangements for his mother's retirement pension. He gets off the train, and while he is having lunch in the hotel, the train leaves without him. He spends the night in the hotel and the following day walks through the deserted streets to the church to attend mass. The priest sees him enter and notices that he is wearing a hat. Recognizing at once that the young man is not one of his parishioners, he decides to dedicate his sermon to him, the subject of which is his recent encounter with the Wandering Jew. Rebeca also attends mass unexpectedly, convinced that Father Antonio Isabel's vision of the Wandering Jew explains why the birds are dying. After delivering his sermon, the priest tells the altar boy to take up the offering, explaining that it will be used to expel the Wandering Jew. He then orders the bewildered child to give the money to the stranger and to tell him he should buy a new hat.

As suggested by the above summary, "One Day After Saturday" is replete with obscure symbolism, most of which is more than likely biblical in origin. The rain of dead birds appears to foreshadow the apocalypse and Christ's reappearance on earth. Although the young stranger seems to be linked to the Wandering Jew, he also apparently represents a Christ figure and thus Macondo's means of salvation in the mind of the senile priest. The new hat he is supposed to receive probably symbolizes the crown Christ will wear as king on earth during the millennium, a replacement for his "crown of thorns," represented by the hat the young man was wearing upon entering the church. Rebeca's return to the church after years of indifference to religion may symbolize the renewal of faith among sinners. The fact that Father Antonio Isabel imagines he sees the Wandering Jew on a Saturday and Christ on the following day perhaps indicates that for him the millennium begins "the day after Saturday."[1]

Although the themes of decadence, madness and solitude are convincingly set forth in this story by the portrait of the priest, the meaning is often clouded by seemingly unfathomable or unrelated episodes. The result is a serious lack of artistic unity and an overall impression of needless obscurity.

Big Mama, the protagonist of "Big Mama's Funeral," is the matriarch of Macondo, whose death sends shock waves not only throughout the nation but even as far away as the Vatican. Her legendary existence, fatal illness, and fabulous burial constitute the story's warp and woof and represent a savage satire on antiquated political, social, and ecclesiastical institutions in Colombia.

"Big Mama's Funeral" utilizes flamboyant rhetorical devices to depict a mythical world in which virtually anything can happen. The narrator reveals himself in the opening lines as a teller of tall tales, a kind of myth chronicler or spokesman for the popular imagination,[2] when he announces his intention of presenting the "true account of Big Mama, absolute sovereign of the kingdom of Macondo, who lived for ninety-two years and died in the odor of sanctity one Tuesday last September, and whose funeral was attended by the pope." This type of narrative perspective enables García Márquez to abandon his former stance of sober neutrality for a variety of styles ranging from whimsical exuberance to concrete simplicity and from pompous exaltation to blunt irreverence. As can be seen in the following description of the funeral's aftermath, the ironic juxtaposition of sharply diverse elements is used to satirize the two principal institutions under attack, the government and the church.

Now that the nation, which was shaken to its vitals, has recovered its balance; now that the bagpipers of San Jacinto, the smugglers of Guajira, the rice planters of Sinú, the prostitutes of Caucamayal, the wizards of Sierpe, and the banana workers of Aracataca, have folded up their tents to recover from the exhausting vigil and have regained their serenity, and the President of the Republic and his ministers and all those who represented the public and supernatural powers on the most magnificent funeral occasion recorded in the annals of history have regained control of their estates; now that the pope has risen up to heaven in body and soul; and now that it is impossible to walk around in Macondo because of the empty bottles, the cigarette butts, the gnawed bones, the tin cans, rags, and excrement that the crowds at the funeral left behind; now is the time to lean a stool against the front door and relate from the beginning the details of this national commotion, before the historians have a chance to get to it.

In the preceding quotation the repetitive *now that* and the proliferation of concrete details (bagpipers, smugglers, rice planters, prostitutes, wizards, banana workers, bottles, cigarette butts, bones, tin cans, rags, etc.) produce a rhythmically hypnotic effect on the reader, inducing him to accept the preposterous exaggerations inserted into the passage ("the most magnificent funeral occasion recorded in the annals of history," "now that the pope has risen up to heaven in body and soul"). The unwary reader is thus lured into an absurd world of ironically balanced contrasts by a variety of stylistic devices that also serve to parody the rhetoric of official pronouncements of the Colombian press.

The decadence of Big Mama's feudal domain is embodied by the doddering priest Father Antonio Isabel as well as by her family, in which "uncles married daughters of their nieces, and cousins married their aunts, and brothers their sisters-in-law, until an intricate mesh of consanguinity was formed, turning procreation into a vicious circle." Her aging doctor is "hostile by philosophical conviction to the progress of his science" and has thus exercised the lifetime privilege granted to him by Big Mama "to prevent the establishment in Macondo of any other physician." Because of arthritis he no longer visits his patients but treats them "by means of supposition, messengers, and errands." When he is finally convinced the matriarch is dying, he applies bloated toads to the site of her pain, leeches to her kidneys, and then "besmeared the dying woman inside and out with all sorts of academic salves, magnificent stimulants, and masterful suppositories."

Until Big Mama was seventy years old her birthdays were always occasions for great rejoicing. Demijohns of rum were placed at the townspeople's disposal

in the central square, cows were butchered, and a band
installed on top of a table would play for three days
without stopping. Stalls were set up that sold "banana
liquor, rolls, blood puddings, chopped fried meat, meat
pies, sausage, yucca breads, doughnuts, buns, corn
breads, puff pastes, tripes, coconut nougats, rum toddies
. . . and scapularies with Big Mama's likeness. . . ." On
the evening of her birthday Big Mama would preside
over a fiesta in her mansion to which were invited
carefully chosen guests and legitimate members of the
family, "generously attended by the bastard line."
After the dancing she would go out on her balcony
and throw coins to the crowd.

Big Mama's death scene is a hilarious example of
grotesque satire. She is first pictured in bed "bedaubed
with aloes up to her ears, under a dust-laden canopy of
oriental crepe." At the moment of administering extreme unction, Father Antonio Isabel is unable to
apply the oils to her palms because the greedy matriarch has her fists tightly clenched to prevent the re-
moval of her rings. During the ensuing struggle with
her nieces she presses her hands to her enormous
breasts and murmurs, "Highway robbers." At dawn
she is seated in her rattan rocker so that she can dic-
tate her will, a process that takes three hours because
her vast holdings comprise three districts and five
townships inhabited by three hundred fifty-two families of tenant farmers.

After her "visible estate" is disposed of she begins
the laborious enumeration of her "invisible estate":
"The wealth of the subsoil, the territorial waters, the
colors of the flag, national sovereignty, the traditional
parties, the rights of man . . . the nation's leadership
. . . congressional hearings . . . free elections . . . the
Supreme Court . . . the meat problem . . . the purity

of the language . . . the Athens of South America*. . .
the lessons of democracy, Christian morality . . . the
Communist menace, the ship of state. . . ." But she is
unable to finish because, "Drowning in the pande-
monium of abstract formulas that for two centuries had
constituted the moral justification of the family's
power, Big Mama emitted a resounding burp and
expired."

The matriarch's obituary and picture as a beautiful young woman appear in special editions of the
nation's major newspapers, where her name is "sancti-
fied by the printed word." The president, realizing the
social order has been "brushed by death" and weighing the "gravity of his responsibility," decrees nine
days of national mourning for the "heroine who had
died for the fatherland on the field of battle." And indeed for many years Big Mama "had guaranteed the
social peace and political harmony of her empire by
virtue of three trunks full of forged electoral certifi-
cates, which formed part of her secret estate. The men
in her service . . . exercised not only their own rights
of suffrage but also those of voters dead for a century."
The funeral is delayed, however, when the courts become involved in the legal question of whether or not
the constitution authorizes the president to leave his
post in the capital in order to attend the ceremony.
Thus, while judges and legislators deliberate for days
and weeks "in the pure atmosphere of the written law,"
and while constitutional amendments are introduced
to permit the president to be present at the burial,
Big Mama's corpse "filled with bubbles in the hot
Macondo September . . . at 104° in the shade."

Meanwhile, the pope has been watching divers

---

* The Colombian capital, Bogotá, is nicknamed the
Athens of Latin America because of its devotion to culture.

search for the head of a decapitated girl in a lake near his summer residence when he sees Big Mama's picture in the newspaper. Recognizing the famous matriarch, he immediately embarks in his canoe for her domain, which is separated from his only by mosquito-infested bogs. Because of the legal deliberations he is obliged to remain for weeks in Macondo's sweltering city hall until one day a priest, accompanied by a drummer, appears in the central square to convey the long-awaited official proclamation: "It was declared . . . ratatatat, and that the President of the Republic, ratatatat, had in his power the extraordinary prerogatives, ratatatat, which permitted him to attend Big Mama's funeral, ratatatat, tatatat, tatat, tatat."

Crowds come from almost everywhere to attend the ceremony, but the most impressive are the political dignitaries, the pope, and the national queens: ". . . the soybean queen, the green-squash queen, the banana queen, the yucca queen, the guava queen, the coconut queen . . . and all the others who are omitted so as not to make this account interminable." As soon as the solemn cortege of grandees departs for the cemetery, Big Mama's heirs literally dismantle her mansion and divide it up among themselves."

The story is rounded off by the narrator's ingenuous assertion that some of the people present were aware of witnessing "the birth of a new era," that now "the pope could ascend to heaven 'in body and soul,'" that the president of the Republic could "govern according to his own good judgment," and that the common people could set up their tents "wherever they damn well pleased in the limitless domain of Big Mama." The narrator's final wish is that the story of Big Mama be told to all those who might doubt it because tomorrow "the garbage men will come and sweep up the trash accumulated during her funeral, forever and ever."

As demonstrated by its authorial detachment, verbal irony, and proper balance of humor and social criticism, "Big Mama's Funeral" is a fine example of political satire. Its fluctuations between grandiose phrases and flippant, sordid details elicit spontaneous mirth from the reader, but, like most satire, its content implies strong passions on the part of the author. Indeed, it represents an acrid critique of his country's semifeudal system fostered by the government in collusion with the church and reactionary landed oligarchy. The apocalyptic vision of Macondo, with all its harsh realities, is intensified by ingenious rhetorical procedures and embellished by flights of fantasy and imagination. The story's ending conveys the optimistic —and perhaps naïve—conviction that the type of social organization depicted is, or soon will be, dead. For its author "Big Mama's Funeral" represents a new brand of realism, a realism expanded and enhanced by magical improbabilities and a keen sense of the grotesque and the absurd.

The eight short stories contained in *Big Mama's Funeral* represent an important segment of García Márquez's total literary work for several reasons. At least four of the tales are outstanding examples of the genre: "Tuesday Siesta," "One of These Days," "Baltazar's Marvelous Afternoon," and the title story. Two of García Márquez's major fictional settings are also depicted in the collection: Macondo, the scene of "Tuesday Siesta," "One Day After Saturday," and "Big Mama's Funeral," and "the town," where the other five stories take place. Though not a primary theme, *la violencia* clearly lurks in the background of "One of These Days" and "Montiel's Widow." In addition, several of García Márquez's most memorable characters appear and reappear in this volume.

Although the literary techniques used in them are basically traditional, these stories represent an interesting variety of short fiction and in some respects reflect the evolution of García Márquez's work in general. For example, in the first pieces of the group ("Tuesday Siesta" and "One of These Days"), the recurring themes of conflicting values and decadence are set forth realistically by a neutral observer. Other tales, such as "Baltazar's Marvelous Afternoon," "Montiel's Widow," and "One Day After Saturday," reveal traces of humor and fantasy that pave the way for "Big Mama's Funeral," by far the funniest and most subjectively conceived story of the collection. The fact that García Márquez chose to entitle his book after this story would seem to indicate its importance in his eyes. Moreover, its placement at the end of the volume in both the Spanish and English editions perhaps signals the overall trend toward fantasy within his fiction.

In its entirety, *Big Mama's Funeral* projects a somber world that nonetheless glistens with subtle psychological apprehensions, striking symbolic images, and occasional infusions of comedy and fancy.

4

Myth and Reality:
The Perfect Synthesis

One Hundred Years of Solitude marks the culmination of García Márquez's literary achievement to date. The universal success of this tragicomic masterpiece is due at least in part to its fascinating plot that can be understood and enjoyed by a large segment of the reading public. The novel tells the complete story of the fictional town of Macondo beginning with its founding by José Arcadio Buendía and his wife Ursula and ending over a century later with its destruction by a devastating hurricane. Because they are cousins, the Buendías live in fear of begetting a child with a pig's tail. Their fear is based on a precedent in the family, a boy with a tail having been born to Ursula's aunt and José Arcadio Buendía's uncle. In García Márquez's fictional world this incident of incest is analogous to "original sin," and seven succeeding generations of Buendías dread the threat of the punishment (the baby with a tail) for this sin. The threat ultimately becomes reality with the love affair between the only remaining Buendías, the scholarly Aureliano Babilonia and his aunt Amaranta Ursula. The solitude referred to in the title emerges as a leitmotif and principal theme, highlighting the characters' irrational single-mindedness and limited capacity for love or meaningful communication in a hostile environment.

After her marriage to José Arcadio Buendía, Ursula, fearful of conceiving a monstrous child, wears a chastity belt to prevent intercourse with her husband until the day he is insulted by one Prudencio Aguilar, who, in a moment of pique, alludes to the still unconsummated union. The impetuous José Arcadio Buendía preserves his honor by killing the man and obliging Ursula to fulfill her conjugal obligations, but Prudencio's ghost soon returns to haunt the couple. Determined to escape from this reminder of the past, the Buendías set out with some of their friends on a long journey through a vast wilderness. More than two years later, exhausted and totally disoriented, José Arcadio Buendía has a dream about a city of houses with mirror walls and convinces his followers to build Macondo on the very spot where they had spent the night.

At first Macondo is a kind of paradise whose idyllically happy inhabitants' only contact with the outside world is provided by roving bands of gypsies exhibiting such fantastic paraphernalia as flying carpets and magnets powerful enough to dislodge pots and pans from the cupboards. Eventually, however, civilization and progress find their way into the community in the form of organized religion, political ideologies, and scientific inventions. Macondo soon becomes involved in a series of bloody civil conflicts. Not long thereafter an American firm, in collaboration with the local authorities, begins to exploit the region's potential for raising bananas. The town is transformed overnight by the arrival of haughty gringos (Americans), who live segregated from the rest of the community, and transient riffraff from other parts of the country. When the dissatisfied workers declare a strike to protest low wages and poor working conditions, the government convenes a meeting in the square opposite the railroad station, allegedly to discuss the terms of an agreement. However, after all exits from the area are cut off by heavily armed soldiers, more than three thousand people are massacred. Almost at once a torrential rain lasting approximately five years begins to fall, bringing an end to economic prosperity and leaving the town in ruins. With the resulting stagnation and exodus of many citizens, it is only a matter of time before Nature completes Macondo's destruction.

The solitude shared by all the Buendías is directly related to their egocentricity, i.e., a tendency to turn inward on themselves rather than outward toward others. This introspection, which partially explains their lack of solidarity with the community, is further illustrated by the recurring threat of incest that haunts each generation and manifests itself in numerous episodes. Although the densely populated novel has no single, clearly defined protagonist, Ursula Buendía probably comes closer to fulfilling this role than any other character. An amazingly practical and energetic woman, she is the clan's mainstay and lives long enough—between 115 and 122 years—to witness most of the events. In contrast to her extraordinary stability, her whimsical husband José Arcadio Buendía is repeatedly carried away by his imagination and eventually goes mad. Other memorable characters include: a mysterious old gypsy named Melquíades who returns from the dead to live in the Buendía household; Pilar Ternera, the mother of two illegitimate children by the sons of José Arcardio Buendía and Ursula; the Buendías' sons, José Arcadio, the prototype of the Latin *macho*, and Colonel Aureliano Buendía, commander of the revolutionary forces during the long civil wars; their daughter Amaranta, an embittered spinster; a foster daughter, Rebeca, who eventually marries José Arcadio; an extraordinarily comely great-granddaughter Remedios the Beauty; her twin brothers José Arcadio Segundo (who takes refuge in madness after witnessing the massacre of the strikers) and the fun-

loving Aureliano Segundo; the latter's prudish wife
Fernanda; their daughters Meme and Amaranta Ursula; and Aureliano Babilonia, the only remaining
member of the clan at the time of the hurricane. (For
a complete Buendía family tree, see page 71.)

A superficial reading of *One Hundred Years of
Solitude* leaves the initial impression of a traditionally
structured work of art, somewhat anachronistic in this
era of avant-garde, experimental literature. Actually
García Márquez has returned to the basic, age-old
methods of telling a story, relying on imagination, fantasy, and episodic adventure to capture a more complete reality than that depicted by the realistic novel
with its strict adherence to mimesis and plausibility.
One Hundred Years of Solitude strives to depict human existence in its totality, i.e., it relates a complex
history—from Eden to Apocalypse—of a family, a
town, an entire world in microcosm, where miracles
such as people riding on flying carpets and a dead man
returning to life tend to erase the line between the subjective and objective realms. The overall impression of
a total fictional universe is further strengthened by the
inclusion of stark tragedy and hilarious humor as well
as by ingeniously conceived stylistic, technical, and
structural devices.

On an historical level, *One Hundred Years of Solitude* presents a vast synthesis of the social, economic,
and political evils that have plagued much of Latin
America since the revolt against Spanish rule early in
the nineteenth century. Even more discernible, however, are the parallels with Colombian reality, the most
obvious being the occasional geographic names and the
episodes dealing with the civil wars and the banana
boom. The novel's temporal sphere remains blurred
because of the complete absence of dates and, at times,
a disregard for chronology. Thus, although numerous
events indicate that the action probably begins in the

THE BUENDÍA FAMILY TREE

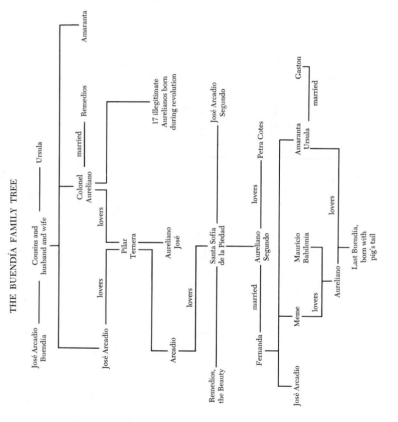

first half of the nineteenth century and ends in the 1920s, we are told that Ursula's great-great-grand-mother was frightened by Sir Francis Drake's attack on Colombia's Atlantic port city of Riohacha, which must have occurred in the late sixteenth century or more than two hundred years before Ursula's birth.

The passages treating the civil wars reflect historic events more accurately. Just before he assumes the leadership of the revolution, Aureliano Buendía is apprised of the issues at stake by the conservative governor, Apolinar Moscote. Though exaggerated for ironic effect, Moscote's words more than likely convey the basic distinctions between the liberal and conservative parties as well as the strong convictions of a conservative leader of the late nineteenth century.

The Liberals . . . were Free Masons, bad people, in favor of hanging priests, of instituting civil marriage and divorce, of recognizing the rights of illegitimate children as equal to those of legitimate ones, and of cutting the country up into a federal system that would take power away from the supreme authorities. The Conservatives, on the other hand, who had received their power directly from God, proposed the establishment of public order and family morality. They were the defenders of the faith of Christ, of the principle of authority, and were not prepared to allow the country to be broken up into autonomous entities.

Having taken up arms against the conservatives because of a fraudulent election, Colonel Aureliano Buendía soon becomes a national legend in spite of the fact that during his twenty years as leader of the revolution he never wins a major battle. At the end of his military career, which can be divided into three phases, he is obliged to recognize the defeat of the liberal cause at the signing of the Treaty of Neerlandia.

Colombian history records that between 1884 and 1902 conservatives and liberals engaged in three civil conflicts—paralleled by the three phases of Colonel

Aureliano Buendía's career—the last being the well-known War of the Thousand Days, brought to an end by the Neerlandia and the Wisconsin Treaties. One of the national heroes of this period was the liberal General Rafael Uribe, under whom García Márquez's grandfather had served and whose career in many respects parallels that of Colonel Aureliano Buendía.[1] Like his fictional counterpart, General Uribe rebelled because of election irregularities and after many years of fighting, signed the Treaty of Neerlandia on behalf of the defeated liberals. Unlike Colonel Aureliano Buendía, who dies in solitary retirement, General Uribe played a prominent role in Colombian politics until his assassination in 1914.

García Márquez's treatment of the banana boom and its disastrous results are also based on historical realities, that is, the arrival of the United Fruit Company in Colombia early in the twentieth century, the years of fabulous prosperity in the author's native Aracataca (Macondo) during World War I, and a massacre of striking banana workers that occurred in 1928 in Ciénaga, a city to the north of Aracataca. An additional parallel between the historical and fictional accounts of the massacre is that in both versions the government authorities exercised tight censorship. Thus, in the novel the facts are never recorded as history, and the tragedy becomes imbedded in the mythical imagination.

García Márquez has said on several occasions that *One Hundred Years of Solitude* is the novel he began to write as a teenager but could not finish for more than twenty years because the appropriate treatment of time always eluded him. He also has stated that as soon as he freed himself from the notion of strict chronology, his most difficult problems were solved. Thus in his masterpiece the lineal history of Macondo's founding, development, economic boom, decline, and de-

struction is imbued with a mytho-poetic atmosphere
of cyclical recurrences and archetypal patterns that
modify temporal progression, establish a more unified
interior structure, and provide a background of greater
thematic and stylistic richness. The nonrational elements of myth also serve to expand the narrow dimensions of objective, everyday reality and lend universal
significance to the experience of the characters.

One Hundred Years of Solitude consists of twenty
unnumbered chapters that can be divided into three
parts in the following manner:

> I   Chapters 1-2
>   Chapter 3 (transition)
> II Chapters 4-15
>   Chapter 16 (transition)
> III Chapters 17-20

Chapters 1 and 2 narrate the beginning of the
Buendía clan; their "original sin" of incest and the
murder of Prudencio Aguilar; their metaphoric return
to the golden age of innocence with the founding of
Macondo; José Arcadio Buendía's awakening to the
wonders of science with the aid of the old gypsy Melquíades; and the arrival in Macondo of merchants and
artisans from the outside world, laying the foundations
for material progress.

The episode of the insomnia plague in chapter 3
is one of the most puzzling and least understood of the
novel. A short time after Rebeca's mysterious arrival
she begins to show symptoms of the strange illness that
not only prevents sleep but, even worse, causes the loss
of memory. Soon people spend their nights amusing
each other with absurd stories like the one about the
capon,

an endless game in which the narrator asked if they wanted
him to tell them the story about the capon, and when they
answered yes, the narrator would say that he had not

asked them to say yes, but whether they wanted him to tell them the story about the capon, and when they answered no, the narrator told them that he had not asked them to say no, but whether they wanted him to tell them the story about the capon, and when they remained silent the narrator told them that he had not asked them to remain silent but whether they wanted him to tell them the story about the capon . . . and so on and on in a vicious circle."

In order not to forget the names and uses of objects, Aureliano Buendía conceives the idea of labeling them, and José Arcadio Buendía, endeavoring to preserve all previously acquired knowledge, builds an ingenious memory machine in the form of a mechanically spinning dictionary. When he has completed approximately 14,000 entries, Melquíades returns to Macondo with a miraculous cure for the illness. The destruction of memory, the efforts to retain human knowledge, and Melquíades's magic potion, convey metaphorically the emergence of Macondo from the status of an archaic, prehistoric community constantly revitalized by the principle of cosmogonic, cyclical renewal to a society characterized by its detachment from nature, its awareness of the historic past, and its acceptance of irreversible lineal time.

Chapters 4 through 15 constitute the portion of the novel most obviously anchored to Colombia's historic reality, the previously mentioned episodes treating the civil wars and the banana boom. These chapters also depict the radical changes that occur in Macondo as a result of scientific progress, economic prosperity, and the corruption of political and humanistic ideals. In chapter 16, a rain lasting four years, eleven months, and two days almost ruins the town, uprooting "every last banana plant" and driving away all but the original inhabitants. Reminiscent of the biblical flood, this storm not only rids Macondo of the gringo imperialists but also effects a temporary spiritual purification through the eradication of decadent materialism, the revival of innocence, and a regeneration of love and mutual understanding. For example, the fabulously rich, hedonistic Aureliano Segundo loses his wealth in the wake of the disaster, while his sexual ardor for Petra Cotes, his mistress, turns to sincere devotion and love. During this time he also delights his daughter and grandson by inventing fantastic tales from the pictures he shows them of historic personages in an English encyclopedia. And in one of the novel's most memorable episodes he endures for almost two days the monotonous, singsong complaining of his wife, Fernanda, about the lack of food in the house before losing his temper and methodically smashing all the glass dishes, china, Bohemian crystal, vases, pictures, and mirrors he can lay his hands on. Having destroyed these symbols of civilization, he throws an oilcloth over his shoulders and goes out to buy food. And after his death, the impoverished Petra Cotes continues her lover's habit of sending baskets of food to Fernanda.

The last four chapters of *One Hundred Years of Solitude* depict the deterioration and ultimate disappearance of Macondo despite scattered efforts to rekindle the virtues and vitality of the past. The tragic ending would seem to result from a variety of factors such as economic depression, irrational self-centeredness, and the stain of original sin that haunts the Buendía clan for so many generations. However, the ravages of time, as reflected by the novel's complex structural design, constitute an additional determinant of the town's fate as well as another major theme.

The above-mentioned cyclical or mythical time offers a temporary escape from the harsh realities of history by rendering the impression of an eternal present, constantly revitalized by recurring configurative patterns. The most obvious case in point is the repetition of names and traits within the Buendía family, the

José Arcadios emerging as impulsive and enterprising, and the Aurelianos as lucid and withdrawn. The plot's cyclical rhythm is also reinforced by the numerous incidents bordering on incest, the most evident involving José Arcadio and Pilar Ternera, a kind of mother figure; Amaranta and her nephew Aureliano José, who returns from the war determined to marry his aunt; Pilar Ternera and her son Arcadio; and Amaranta and her decadent great-great-nephew José Arcadio, who drowns in his bath "still thinking about Amaranta." These episodes not only help to sustain dramatic momentum but also foreshadow the apocalyptic denouement by keeping alive the myth of original sin.

Another means of escape from lineal into mythical time is provided by the development of the plot in a series of circularly composed units, allowing for frequent repetitions and conveying a floating, spiral effect. One of many examples is the opening sentence of the first chapter. "Many years later, as he faced the firing squad, Colonel Aureliano Buendía was to remember that distant afternoon when his father took him to discover ice." Here the allusion to a future occurrence (Colonel Aureliano Buendía facing the firing squad) is followed by an abrupt shift to a past event (the discovery of ice), which in turn becomes the climactic incident at the end of the chapter.

Both mythical and historical functions are fulfilled by many of the characters, the most important being Ursula, Melquíades, Colonel Aureliano Buendía, and José Arcadio Buendía. An archetypal representation of the wise and energetic matriarch, Ursula does her utmost to bolster family unity, ward off the curse of incest, and prevent injustice. Her quest for permanence and stability in a world increasingly menaced by chaos is underscored by her acute awareness of the cyclical nature of time. Thus, as she observes the irrational behavior reappearing in each generation of her

descendants, her oft-repeated statement that time is
not passing but turning in a circle does not necessarily
convey despair but rather an illusion of a perpetual
present. Her own actions also emphasize the principle of regeneration as exemplified by her repeated
renovations of the Buendía home, the first time in order
that Amaranta and Rebeca can entertain their young
friends, again at the end of the civil wars, and finally
after the rains have ceased. Each effort, however, is
less effective because of her advancing years. Her
death on Good Friday between the age of 115 and 122
is surrounded by a series of strange occurrences that
harbinger disaster for Macondo but at the same time
lend mythical dimensions to her heroic existence: luminous orange discs pass across the sky, birds break
through window screens during the midday heat and
die inside the houses, and on Easter Sunday the hun-
dred-year-old priest announces he has seen a monster
whom he claims to be the legendary Wandering Jew.

Ursula, however, is also very much a part of the
historical time frame. Early in the novel she leaves
Macondo in search of her wayward son José Arcadio,
finds her way to civilization, and returns with new settlers whose technical skills contribute much to the
town's material progress. She exhibits a flair for making
money, establishing a prosperous candy business while
her husband immerses himself in a variety of impractical projects in his laboratory. And her openmindedness
to other cultures and changing customs is manifested
by her warm hospitality to outsiders and her willing-
ness to allow her great-great-granddaughter Meme to
accept the social invitations extended to her by the
gringos.

As the years pass, Ursula begins to sense "everyday reality slipping through her hands" and gradually
comes to realize that "the progressive disruption of
time" is her worst enemy. In spite of her astonishing

will to survive, her frustrations due to blindness and old age make her increasingly aware of the lack of meaning in her existence. Her situation reaches the height of the absurd during the rains when, shrunken and failing mentally, she becomes a toy for her mischievous great-great-great-granddaughter Amaranta Ursula and her great-great-great-great-grandson Aureliano Babilonia. They paint her face, dress her in ludicrous clothing and even hide her in the pantry where she is almost eaten by rats. After the rains she makes a brief but valiant effort to restore order to the household, but she soon loses contact with reality, begins to live in the distant past, and finally falls victim to the lineal time she has resisted all her life.

The gypsy Melquíades, another composite of mythical and human elements, is described at the beginning of the novel as "a fugitive from all the plagues in Persia, scurvy in the Malayan archipelago, leprosy in Alexandria, beriberi in Japan, bubonic plague in Madagascar, an earthquake in Sicily, and a shipwreck in the Straits of Magellan." He is also presented as "a prodigious creature . . . enveloped in a sad aura, with an Asiatic look that seemed to know what there was on the other side of things." His dress includes a large black hat resembling a raven with widespread wings and a velvet vest "across which the patina of the centuries had skated." He is endowed with an immense and mysterious wisdom but suffers from down-to-earth problems such as the ailments of old age and financial burdens. And he never laughs because scurvy has caused his teeth to drop out.

Melquíades reappears in Macondo on one occasion miraculously rejuvenated by a set of false teeth. Years later, having died and become bored with the solitude of death, he returns to live with the Buendías in a room built especially for him. It is here that he spends the rest of his life writing his enigmatic manuscripts on sheets of parchment in an unknown language. After his second death his spirit comes back to converse with the members of the Buendía clan who attempt to decipher his work. For many years his room remains invulnerable to the passing of time, preserving the magic aura of a permanent present and protecting its inhabitants from adverse events. Inasmuch as his manuscript and the novel turn out to be one and the same, Melquíades emerges not only as the narrator, but also as an archetype of mythical omniscience. He fulfills an historical function as well, for it is he who introduces the wonders of science to José Arcadio Buendía and inspires him to seek progress through knowledge. Finally, it will be recalled that Melquíades's cure for the insomnia plague brings about Macondo's permanent detachment from nature and propulsion into the course of history.

Although Colonel Aureliano Buendía is the novel's most historically based figure and ultimately reveals certain characteristics of the twentieth-century absurd man, he too occasionally takes on the aura of myth. He is said to have wept in his mother's womb, to have been born with his eyes open, and at the age of three predicts that a pot of soup will fall moments before it slides to the edge of the table and crashes to the floor. His powers of clairvoyance also enable him to foresee his father's death before it actually happens. Though apolitical prior to the civil war, he joins the revolt of the liberals ostensibly to stem political corruption on the part of the conservatives. His struggle for justice becomes legendary as a result of the thirty-two armed uprisings he leads, the fourteen unsuccessful attempts made against his life, and his escape from the seventy-three ambushes and one firing squad. His odyssey through the Caribbean also represents a metaphoric, internalized journey to disillusion and solitude as illustrated by his gradual repudiation of liberal ideals, his preposterous isolation inside a circle of chalk for protection against would-be assassins, and his tyrannical conduct. Shortly before the end of the war he admits he is fighting only for power, "wallowing like a hog in a dunghill of glory." Eventually he comes to the cynical conclusion that the only difference between the liberals and the conservatives is that the former attend mass at five o'clock and the latter at eight o'clock.

Like the absurd man of modern existential literature, Colonel Aureliano Buendía becomes acutely aware of the disproportion between his intentions and reality. Unlike the absurd hero, however, he ultimately abandons the struggle, retires to his workshop, and devotes himself to making little gold fishes, selling them for gold coins, and converting the coins back into gold fishes. This fruitless routine recalls that of Sisyphus, the mythical character whom Albert Camus has described as the epitome of the absurd hero. But a major difference exists between Colonel Aureliano Buendía and Sisyphus—the colonel ends his life in tragic solitude and defeat whereas Sisyphus gives joy and meaning to his existence by defying the gods and fulfilling his task of rolling a stone up a hill again and again for eternity.

The colonel's status as an historically oriented character is further evidenced by the fact that he alone among the Buendías fails to see Melquíades's room as a mythical realm of timelessness, being aware only of the dust and debris that have accumulated there over the years. On the last day of his life his alienation is expressed symbolically when he falls asleep in his hammock and dreams of entering an empty house with white walls. That same afternoon he hears a circus parade passing by the house, and from the front door he sees a woman dressed in gold sitting on the head of an elephant, a sad dromedary, and a bear dressed like a Dutch girl keeping time to the music with a soup spoon and a pan. When the procession finally comes to an end, he finds himself contemplating his "miserable solitude" mirrored in the expanse of the street where a few onlookers are still "peering over the precipice of uncertainty."

Colonel Aureliano Buendía dies minutes later while urinating under the chestnut tree in the patio with his head tucked in between his shoulders "like a baby chick." His body is not discovered until the following day when circling vultures draw attention to it. Thus, unlike Ursula, whose mytho-poetic death pays tribute to her mortal achievements, the colonel dies utterly alone, the absurdity of his life conveyed by the passing circus, and of his death, by the carrion-eating vultures. And only two generations later the last surviving Buendía discovers that the colonel's heroic exploits during the civil wars have been erased from the collective memory of Macondo.

In his delineation of Macondo's restless, energetic patriarch, García Márquez alludes to mythical and historic realities that reflect basic aspects of the evolving human condition and at the same time prefigure the novel's denouement. José Arcadio Buendía's dream about a noisy city of mirror-walled houses on the eve of the founding of Macondo represents not only a version of the creation myth but also his illusions about the unlimited extent of human potential. His exposure to alchemy and astrology by Melquíades recalls the legendary relationship between Faust and Mephistopheles during the middle ages. Melquíades's cure of the insomnia plague (José Arcadio Buendía is the first to receive the potion) assures Macondo's entrance into the stream of historic time, and the invention of photography inspires the skeptical founder to make use of the camera in his attempts to prove the existence of God. Soon thereafter he becomes fascinated with the intricate design of a mechanical ballerina, a metaphor of the eighteenth-century, deistic concept of a rational, perfectly ordered universe. His subsequent conversations with the ghost of Prudencio Aguilar, who is terrified of dying a second death, expand the dimensions of his perception of reality and signal his excursion into the absurd labyrinth of time and space representing the twentieth-century view of the world. Increasingly frustrated by the chaos he encounters, José Arcadio Buendía declares that "the time machine has broken down" and succumbs to an attack of madness. He is then tied to a huge chestnut tree in the courtyard, where he remains for many years chattering in Latin "in a state of total innocence." At the moment of his death he envisions himself lost in a labyrinth of identical rooms resembling "a gallery of parallel mirrors." The preparations for his funeral are interrupted by a rain of tiny yellow flowers that inundate the streets of Macondo. Shortly after his burial his ghost appears on the patio to chat with members of the family.

Thus, in death José Arcadio Buendía, like his wife Ursula, transcends the physical and the commonplace through the intensity of his solitary, lifelong struggle to unravel the mysteries of the universe. The significance of his achievements becomes evident through his emergence as a universal archetype, his mythical stature having been assured by his Promethean fate of being tied to the chestnut tree (Prometheus was enchained for defying the laws of the gods), the fantastic rain of flowers proclaiming his death, and the return of his ghost to preserve his descendants' memory of him as the founding patriarch. The overall evolution of his outlook on life, moreover, is illustrated by the contrast between his dream as a young man inspiring him to build a glittering utopian society and, just before he dies, his vision of the labyrinth, a metaphor of contemporary man's nonrational concept of the world, i.e., a world in which the limits of reason have illuminated the absurdity of the human condition.

In spite of the purifying effects of the rains, which have brought an end to the banana boom, death soon takes all but two of the remaining Buendías, and Macondo's decline continues unabated. While plants and insects invade the rooms where Amaranta Ursula and Aureliano Babilonia make passionate, incestuous love, Pilar Ternera metaphorically describes the history of the Buendía clan, and the novel's temporal mechanism, as "a machine with unavoidable repetitions, a turning wheel that would have gone on spinning into eternity were it not for the progressive and irremediable wearing of the axle." The turning wheel of the time machine would seem to symbolize cyclical recurrence, and the axle, lineal history, the crushing weight of which has undermined the rhythm of mythical renewal and brought the fictional world to a state of entropy.

Pilar Ternera's insight becomes reality when Amaranta Ursula bleeds to death, her monstrous child is eaten by ants, and Aureliano Babilonia, realizing that his own fate must be revealed in Melquíades's writings, encloses himself in the old gypsy's quarters, never to emerge again. He finds the parchments intact "among the prehistoric plants . . . and luminous insects that had removed all traces of man's passage on earth from the room" and at last manages to read the mysterious language (Sanskrit) as if it were his native tongue. Thus he starts to decipher the entire history of the Buendía family, fascinated by the sequence of events beginning with Sir Francis Drake's attack on Riohacha in order that he, Aureliano Babilonia, and his aunt Amaranta Ursula could seek each other "through the most intricate labyrinth of blood" and engender the "mythological animal" that would bring the line to an end. He soon discovers, however, that instead of chronicling the events in conventional, lineal time, Melquíades has compressed a century of daily occurrences in such a way that they coexist in one instant. As he feverishly continues his task, a warm wind "full of voices from the past" makes itself heard, little by little acquiring the force of a "biblical hurricane." Minutes later while translating the present moment of his life, "as if he were looking into a speaking mirror," he realizes his fate is sealed:

for it was foreseen that the city of mirrors (or mirages) would be wiped out by the wind and exiled from the memory of men at the precise moment when Aureliano Babilonia would finish deciphering the parchments, and that everything written on them was unrepeatable since time immemorial and forever more, because races condemned to one hundred years of solitude did not have a second opportunity on earth.

The novel's last three pages are extremely important to its overall meaning. As the narrator, Melquíades is probably García Márquez's Muse. The ancient Indo-European Sanskrit would seem to represent language in general and thus an appropriate vehicle for recording universal human experiences. The complete history of the Buendía family emerges as another version of the labyrinth, but unlike José Arcadio Buendía, whose frustrating confrontation with chaotic reality leads to his madness, Aureliano Babilonia successfully finds his way through the maze to discover both his unknown origin and his destiny. A major difference between the quests of José Arcadio Buendía and Aureliano Babilonia is that the former penetrates the labyrinth of real life, with all its unpredictable temporal and spatial incoherence, whereas the latter unravels the artificial complexities of an artistically fashioned, fictitious paradigm of reality, perhaps man's only perfect foil to disorder and nothingness.

One may wonder, then, why Melquíades's impec-

cably structured world must perish. José Arcadio
Buendía's dream about a city of mirror-walled houses
conveys a mistaken confidence in man's perfectability
because it fails to take into account the seeds of evil he
carries within himself in the form of original sin. Moreover, art, like an object reflected in a mirror, is not the
thing it represents but a mere illusion, a recreation of
an ideal reality, as demonstrated so graphically by
Melquíades's concentration of a century of daily episodes into one magic instant outside the boundaries of
time and space. This metaphor of aesthetic perfection
is swept away almost at once by the terrifying winds
of history, implying somewhat ironically that even the
citadel of art cannot withstand twentieth-century man's
destructive capabilities.

Still, Macondo's tragic fate is perhaps best explained not by philosophical conjecture, but by artistic
motives. García Márquez has stated on several occasions that he would like to have been a magician rather
than a writer. This preference can be detected in *One
Hundred Years of Solitude*, a total world of pure fiction ingeniously conceived and destroyed from within
by legerdemain, as if its real creator were invisible or
nonexistent. And equally remarkable, this all-encompassing, self-contained world includes even its reader
who finds himself trapped within its steadily shrinking
boundaries and destined to be carried off by the holo-
caust. Indeed, there is evidence that Aureliano Babilonia represents Melquíades's alter ego or García Márquez's ideal reader. This author-reader relationship is
suggested at the beginning of Chapter 18, when we are
told that Aureliano Babilonia is a medieval scholar
who, like Melquíades, possesses a vast knowledge of
the world outside Macondo despite the fact that he
has spent his life as a virtual hermit. Soon after his
conversation with Melquíades, in which he is told to
obtain a Sanskrit grammar in order to decode the

parchments, the old gypsy announces his last death. Almost immediately, his room falls prey to the heat, dust, and insects already invading the rest of the house. Having left his quarters for the local bookshop on several occasions, Aureliano Babilonia also begins to take an interest in Macondo, making friends with some of the town citizens and observing its accelerating decline. The horrible fate of the child precipitates his return to the parchments because Melquíades's epigraph had provided him with a clue to the contents: "The first of the line is tied to a tree and the last is being eaten by ants." Thus Aureliano Babilonia hastens to Melquíades's room, nails the doors and windows shut, and immerses himself in the Buendía family chronicle, utterly oblivious to the outside world. The hurricane filled with voices of the past conveys metaphorically the torrent of words he is translating; and the "speaking mirror," into which he gazes upon reaching the last page, implies his perfect communication with his double, Melquíades. This ideal communication between the writer and his reader becomes, then, an integral part of the total fictional universe at the very moment of its obliteration.[2]

García Márquez's skillful fusion of reality and fantasy is another means by which his novel renders the impression of a total fictional world in which anything is possible and everything can appear real.[3] An anecdote he tells about one of his aunts provides a clue to his narrative technique. It seems that this aunt was always consulted whenever an explanation for any strange occurrence was needed, and what impressed García Márquez most was her ability to convince people of the truth of her absurd replies. He recalls that one day a child approached her with an oddly shaped egg and asked her why it was so peculiar. The aunt examined it carefully and answered, "Look, you want to know why this egg has this bulge? Well, because it's

a basilisk egg. Light a fire in the patio." So they built
the fire and burned the egg as if it were the most natural thing in the world to do. "This 'naturalness,'" García Márquez states, "gave me the key to *One Hundred
Years of Solitude*, in which the most frightful, the most
unusual, things are told with the same dead-pan expression my aunt had when they burned the basilisk
egg on the patio, without ever even knowing what it
was."[4]

Numerous episodes in the novel illustrate the
writer's adroit manipulation of language and narrative
focus for the purpose of fusing the real and fantastic
elements of his fictional world. A case in point is his
treatment of the mysterious death of José Arcadio, the
older son of José Arcadio Buendía and Ursula. One day
José Arcadio returns from a hunting trip to the home
he shares with his wife, Rebeca. After tying up his dogs
in the courtyard and leaving a string of dead rabbits
in the kitchen to be salted, he goes into the bedroom to
change his clothes. Moments later the sound of a pistol
shot signals his death and its strange aftermath.

A trickle of blood came out under the door, crossed the
living room, went out into the street, continued on in a
straight line across the uneven terraces, went down steps
and climbed over curbs, passed along the Street of the
Turks, turned a corner to the right and another to the
left, made a right angle at the Buendía house, went in
under the closed door, crossed through the parlor, hugging
the walls so as not to stain the rugs, went on to the other
living room, made a wide curve to avoid the dining-room
table, went along the porch with the begonias, and passed
without being seen under Amaranta's chair as she gave
an arithmetic lesson to Aureliano José, and went through
the pantry and came out in the kitchen, where Ursula was
getting ready to crack thirty-six eggs to make bread.

"Holy mother of God!" Ursula shouted.

Equally remarkable is Ursula's subsequent revelation that the flow of blood comes from the victim's right ear and that no weapon or wound on his body is to be found. José Arcadio's death is utterly absurd, but it is made almost believable by the meticulous stylistic precision, down-to-earth language, and numerous everyday details surrounding the occurrence.

The opposite effect is realized by the description of José Arcadio Buendía's discovery of ice when he takes his two young sons to the circus. He first asks the gypsies about Melquíades and is deeply distressed to learn that his old friend has succumbed to the fever in Singapore and been buried in the deepest part of the Java Sea. José Arcadio Buendía's children insist that he take them to a nearby tent, which supposedly had belonged to King Solomon, in order to see the so-called "novelty of the sages of Memphis." After purchasing three tickets, they enter the tent in which a giant gypsy with a copper ring in his nose and a heavy iron chain on his ankle opens a pirate chest containing the "novelty."

Inside there was only an enormous, transparent block with infinite internal needles in which the light of the sunset was fragmented into colored stars. Disconcerted, knowing that the children were waiting for an immediate explanation, José Arcadio Buendía ventured a murmur,

"It's the largest diamond in the world."

"No," the gypsy countered. "It's ice."

Having paid an additional fee, José Arcadio Buendía

put his hand on the ice and held it there for several minutes as his heart filled with fear and jubilation at the contact with mystery. . . . Intoxicated with the evidence of the miracle, he forgot at that moment about . . . Melquíades's body, abandoned to the appetite of the squids. He paid another five reales, and with his hand on the block of ice, as if giving testimony on the holy scriptures, exclaimed

"This is the greatest invention of our time."

In this passage an ordinary object (ice) is imbued with an aura of magic by the imaginative, emotion-packed language and wealth of exotic details setting the stage for José Arcadio Buendía's intense reactions to the "mystery." García Márquez's treatment of José Arcadio's death and José Arcadio Buendía's discovery of ice illustrates his method of making the fantastic seem real and the real fantastic, thus eliminating the barrier between objective and imaginary realities and creating a total fictional universe. The role of the practical-minded Ursula in the first episode lends a note of down-to-earth realism to her son's incredible death, just as her flighty husband's role in the second episode changes ice into an object of wonder. One can only conclude that reality is relative, elusive, and at times even contradictory, its authenticity depending on the eyes of the viewer or the vantage point from which it is presented.

Some readers find *One Hundred Years of Solitude* tragic and depressing because its characters seem condemned by their hostile environment to frustration, solitude, and despair. There is, indeed, in the novel a veritable litany of poignant moments that tend to convey a chaotic, fragmentary world in which loneliness and pain appear to be the only constants. Still, this bleak panorama of life is frequently enlivened by infusions of fantasy and humor, ranging from madcap hilarity and hyperbolic absurdities to sophisticated irony. The resultant blurring of sharp distinction creates a tragicomic reality, broader in scope and richer in ambiguity.

For many years Macondo accepts the fantastic as an integral part of life without showing any signs of disbelief or amazement at such remarkable phenomena as the canvas sack containing the bones of Rebeca's parents that make a "cloc-cloc-cloc sound" until they are finally buried; Melquíades's return from death because he cannot bear the solitude; Father Nicanor Reyna's proof of God's existence by levitating six inches off the ground upon drinking a cup of hot chocolate; and the fabulous proliferation of Aureliano Segundo's animals resulting from the mere presence of his mistress Petra Cotes on his breeding grounds. However, the arrival of technology in the form of trains, electric lights, the movies, the phonograph, and the telephone cause havoc among the inhabitants of the town who no longer know for certain "where the limits of reality lay." Thus the train resembles "a kitchen dragging a village behind it"; the movies emerge as an "outlandish fraud" because an actor dies in one film and appears again in another as somebody else; the phonograph seems to be nothing more than a mechanical trick to amuse children; and because of its crank the telephone is simply a rudimentary version of the phonograph.

Perhaps the most diverting example of fantasy is the rise heavenward of Remedios the Beauty, an incident often compared to the Assumption of the Virgin Mary. The girl's fabulous physical attractions include not only her comely face and body, but also her tormenting "breath of perturbation" or "fatal emanation" so disturbing to members of the opposite sex. Her beauty causes the death or ruination of at least four men, one of whom resembles the typical fairy-tale prince, "riding a horse with silver stirrups and a velvet blanket." Prior to her ascension Remedios the Beauty is described somewhat mischievously as not being a creature of this world, her habits revealing her innocence, lack of inhibitions, and complete disregard for conventions. She shaves her head, wanders naked through the house at the age of twenty and, if not watched carefully, is likely to paint little animals on the walls with a stick daubed in her own excrement. One day while she is folding Fernanda's sheets in the garden a wind suddenly comes up and carries her skyward along with the flapping linens. Though outsiders suspect the "tale of levitation" has been fabricated to conceal an act of "immoral" behavior, most townspeople eventually accept the miracle and even light candles and celebrate novenas. Fernanda, however, cannot forget the loss of her fine sheets and keeps praying for their return.

García Márquez's humor relies heavily on hyperbole and preposterous distortions, occasionally creating a tone of high comedy that marks him as a practitioner of absurd literature. Thus, through the negation of reason and logic he probes the other side of existence in order to reveal the disproportion between human intentions and reality. Some of the more notable examples of the resultant Rabelaisian exuberance and ludicrous exaggeration include Aureliano Buendía's courtship of the nine-year-old Remedios Moscote, who still wets the bed and has yet to reach puberty at the time of their engagement; the hilarious parody of the *machismo* myth presented in the character of José Arcadio, whose unprecedented strength and virility make him the prize for a raffle among the prostitutes at the local brothel; the appearance at the Buendía home of Colonel Aureliano Buendía's seventeen sons, all by different women and all with "a look of solitude" that leaves no doubt about their relationship to the family; the confused identities of the twins Aureliano Segundo and Arcadio Segundo during their childhood and again when they are buried in the wrong graves by "sad drunkards"; the gringos' divine powers to alter the rain cycles and unleash storms; the fabulous three-day eating contest between Aureliano

Segundo and his victorious adversary "The Elephant," a charming, impeccably groomed music-school director who, among other things, consumes the juice of forty oranges, eight quarts of coffee, thirty raw eggs, two pigs, a bunch of bananas, and four cases of champagne; and Pilar Ternera's death at the age of 145 and her burial in a rocking chair under the dance floor of her fabulous brothel decorated with live tropical birds and crocodiles.

Fernanda del Carpio, the beautiful, straitlaced aristocrat from the mountainous interior and wife of Aureliano Segundo, is the butt of many amusing episodes, some absurd and others bordering on black humor and the grotesque.* Born and raised in a distant, gloomy city where "the coaches of viceroys still rattled through the cobbled streets on ghostly nights," she has been convinced by her parents that her family is immensely rich and that some day she, like her great-grandmother, will be a queen. In reality, when she completes her convent education, Fernanda is obliged to weave funeral wreaths in order to help keep the family economically solvent. She first goes to Macondo as a beauty queen, sent by the conservative government for devious political motives. Soon after her departure for her native city, the enamored Aureliano Segundo travels inland, over mountains and across plateaus, in search of the "most beautiful woman who had ever been seen on this earth." His fairy-tale journey comes to an end when Fernanda accepts his proposal and returns to Macondo with several trunkloads of heirlooms and her golden chamberpot bearing the family crest. According to the calendar

---

* Fernanda's presence in Macondo highlights the very real difference in moral and social attitudes between the carefree inhabitants of the Colombian coastal region and the more conservative highlanders.

given to her by her spiritual adviser, all but forty-two days out of the year are marked as dates of "venereal abstinence." Two weeks after the wedding, when Aureliano Segundo finally enters her bedroom to consummate the marriage, he is unable to suppress an explosion of laughter upon seeing his wife in an ankle-length nightgown with long sleeves and "a large, round buttonhole, delicately trimmed, at the level of her lower stomach."

To her children Fernanda has always painted an idealized portrait of their grandfather, Don Fernando, creating in their minds the image of a pious, legendary being. Every year for Christmas he sends the family a large box of mementos from the ancestral home that the children await with great anticipation. One December day an enormous lead chest arrives addressed to the Very Distinguished Lady Doña Fernanda del Carpio de Buendía. When Aureliano Segundo finally manages to break the seal and raises the lid for the excited youngsters, they are confronted with Don Fernando in the flesh, "dressed in black and with a crucifix on his chest, his skin broken out in pestilential sores and cooking slowly in a frothy stew with bubbles like live pearls."

Many years later Fernanda suffers from a uterine disorder, but too modest to see a doctor in person, she initiates a long correspondence with her "invisible physicians" who eventually prescribe a telepathic operation. Thus, at the date and hour agreed upon she lies down in her room with her head pointed north and feels her face being covered with a handkerchief soaked in a "glacial liquid." Upon awakening several hours later, she has a "barbarous line of stitches in the shape of an arc that began at her groin and ended at her sternum."

Another example of humor derived from hyperbole occurs when Meme, Fernanda's daughter, unex-

pectedly returns from boarding school, accompanied
by sixty-eight schoolmates and four nuns to spend a
week's vacation with the family. Their arrival throws
the entire household into chaos, one of the problems
being the nocturnal congestion in the bathroom. Fernanda endeavors to alleviate the situation with the
purchase of seventy-two chamber pots, but this plan
backfires because her guests then line up in the morning to wash out the utensils. Chaos almost turns to
panic when one of the nuns who happens into the
kitchen asks Amaranta what ingredient she is adding
to the soup and receives the sharp reply, "Arsenic."

Amaranta's demise, like that of her brother José
Arcadio, constitutes another absurd episode narrated
in utter seriousness. Four years before she dies she is
visited by death in the form of a woman dressed in
blue who tells her that she should begin sewing her
shroud on the sixth of April and that she will die at
dusk on the day she finishes it. Amaranta's long period
of labor evokes Penelope's strategem to deceive her
would-be suitors and remain faithful to Ulysses, but
unlike her mythical counterpart, Amaranta nurtures
solitude instead of love. At eight o'clock one morning
she takes the last stitch in "the most beautiful piece
of work that any woman had ever finished" and announces that she is going to die at dusk. A carpenter
is summoned to take the measurements for her coffin.
In the aftrenoon she bathes, dresses, braids her hair
and lies down to await the end. In the meanwhile her
offer to act as courier for anybody wishing to send letters to the dead has attracted a flood of messages that
are collected in a sealed box to be placed in her grave.
During the final moments of her life, she rejects the
priest's offer for spiritual aid, preferring to boast of her
virginity: "Let nobody have any illusions . . . Amaranta
Buendía is leaving this world just as she came into it."
The irony of this statement uttered just before her

death is heightened by the fact that her name evokes the very qualities she lacked most throughout her long life (*amar* means to love in Spanish).

Not infrequently the eruption of the preposterous or the grotesque in the midst of serious narration furnishes comic relief and ironic contrast. For example, the early history of the Buendía family includes an incident involving Ursula's great-great-grandmother who became so frightened during Sir Francis Drake's attack on Riohacha that she lost control of her nerves and sat on a lighted stove. From that time on she could only sit on one side, cushioned by pillows, and "something strange must have happened to her way of walking, for she never walked in public again." In a somewhat similar fashion a demonstration of modern dance given during a fiesta in the Buendía home is disrupted by a fight, with biting and hair-pulling, between Pilar Ternera and a woman who remarks that Arcadio (Pilar Ternera's son) has a feminine derrière.

After the civil wars, Colonel Aureliano Buendía becomes so immersed in making gold fishes that he loses interest in political news such as the reform of the calendar in order that every president can remain in power for a hundred years, a picture of the liberal ministers kneeling before a cardinal sent from Rome to sign the concordat (an agreement between the papacy and the government), and the kidnapping by masked highwaymen of a Spanish theatrical company's leading lady who danced nude the following Sunday at the president's summer house. During the riotous jubilee celebrated in honor of Colonel Aureliano Buendía, all seventeen of his sons arrive unexpectedly to spend three days with the family. Among other things, they smash half of the dishes, make Remedios the Beauty put on a pair of men's pants and climb a greased pole, and turn loose in the dining room a pig daubed with lard, prostrating Fernanda. When Fernanda first learns from a nun of her illegitimate grandson's existence, she regrets that the medieval custom of hanging the messenger of bad tidings has been abandoned. And toward the end of the novel, as Aureliano Babilonia wanders through the ruins of the banana-company town, he hears a telephone ringing, picks up the receiver, and tells an anguished, English-speaking woman that the strike is over, the gringos have left, and peace has finally come to Macondo.

Because of its depiction of Yankee imperialism, the episode of the strike is the most reminiscent of social-protest literature. The injection of humor and fantasy into this important incident, however, while in no way diminishing the implied condemnation of foreign exploitation, enhances the novel's aesthetic worth and makes it far more enjoyable than objective realism. It also parodies historical narrative and mocks official lies by inflating them *ad absurdum.* The banana workers become dissatisfied because they are not paid in real money but in scrip that will only buy Virginia ham sold in the company commissaries. Whether they are suffering from malaria, gonorrhea, or constipation, sick employees are given pills the color of copper sulfate that children collect and use for bingo markers. Another source of complaint is that instead of installing plumbing facilities in the miserable barracks built for the workers, the company engineers are accustomed to bringing portable latrines to the camps at Christmas time and holding public demonstrations on how to use them so that they will last longer.

When the strikers formulate a list of demands, Mr. Brown and the other leading representatives of the banana firm suddenly disappear from Macondo. Then, in order to foil the strikers and cloud the issue, the company lawyers produce Mr. Brown's death certificate "proving" that he has been run over by a fire engine in Chicago. The workers eventually take their case to a higher court only to be told by the "sleight-of-hand lawyers" that their demands have no validity. It seems that the banana company does not have, never has had, and never will have any workers in its service because they have all been hired on a temporary basis and therefore, by solemn decree of the court, "the workers did not exist."

The massacre is made less brutal but all the more vivid by several factors. The metaphoric language poetizes the tragic scene, creating sharp visual imagery characteristic of a surrealistic dream: ". . . the panic became a dragon's tail . . . swirling about in a gigantic whirlwind that little by little was being reduced to its epicenter as the edges were systematically being cut off all around like an onion being peeled by the insatiable and methodical shears of the machine guns."

Fiction and reality become confused with the gratuitous appearance of Colonel Lorenzo Gavilán, one of the strike leaders but originally a character from *The Death of Artemio Cruz* by the Mexican novelist Carlos Fuentes. Furthermore, some of the events are shorn of the impact of immediacy by being filtered through the mind of a child who witnesses the killing and many years later relates what he recalls. Finally, an eerie, nightmarish feeling is generated when the wounded Arcadio Segundo regains consciousness on a two-hundred-car freight train loaded with corpses, jumps off, and makes his way back to Macondo, where he is assured that nothing has happened. The entire incident soon becomes shrouded in myth, as evidenced by Arcadio Segundo's fate. Obsessed by his terrifying experience and fearful of being arrested for his role as one of the strike leaders, he takes refuge in the pure, timeless atmosphere of Melquíades's room. A short time later a group of soldiers searches the house, but when the officer in command peers through the door to the spot where Arcadio Segundo is waiting to be led away, he sees only the havoc wrought by years of neglect. Although Arcadio Segundo eventually loses his mind and never leaves Melquíades's room again, he passes his knowledge of the strike on to Aureliano Babilonia, who discovers it to be radically different from the version created for the school books.

One Hundred Years of Solitude is replete with irony, an element that not only lends subtle humor and comic relief to a work of art, but also enhances its structural unity by juxtaposing incompatibles, balancing opposites, and creating dramatic tension. An ironic view of reality, moreover, often represents the only possible response of the artist to an ambiguous world fraught with disorder and uncertainty. Examples abound. Unable to reach the sea, José Arcadio Buendía founds Macondo in the wilderness, but later when he sets out in search of "civilization," he finds the sea. Ursula leaves Macondo to bring back her son who ran off with a band of gypsies and discovers the route sought by her husband. She refuses to be photographed because she does not want "to survive as a laughingstock for her grandchildren," but toward the end of her days she receives the brunt of the most grotesque practical jokes imaginable. The people of Macondo are oblivious to sin until Father Nicanor Reyna arrives to marry Rebeca and Pietro Crespi and discovers the necessity of planting "the seed of God" among them. Years later he converses with José Arcadio Buendía in Latin under the chestnut tree, attempting to "inject the faith into his twisted mind," but the old patriarch's lucid rationalism threatens to undermine the priest's religious convictions. Colonel Aureliano Buendía cannot understand how people can go to the extreme of waging war over abstract ideas until he becomes entangled in a chain of events that makes him just as brutal and despotic as his worst enemies. Eventually he fights only for self-liberation and manages "to win a defeat much more difficult . . . than victory." The day he signs the Treaty of Neerlandia he is vilified by the people of Macondo, but when his suicide attempt backfires, he regains his former prestige overnight, having become a martyr of the revolution.

During the last days of the civil war, three unknown men leave in the Buendía home an enormous plaster statue of Saint Joseph that Ursula stands in a corner to await the owners' return. Years later when Macondo achieves affluence from the banana boom and Aureliano Segundo initiates his hedonistic escapades, Ursula begs God to make them poor and virtuous again. Her prayers are answered in reverse, however, when the statue is accidentally broken and almost four hundred pounds of gold coins spill out onto the floor. Ursula is particularly mortified because she has been putting candles on the saint and prostrating herself before it without being aware of its contents. She hastily buries the money in a secret place where it remains hidden until the last José Arcadio discovers it and converts the house into a decadent paradise.

The ironic juxtaposition of opposites is often a source of the dynamic narrative movement characterizing the novel. For example, the diverting and fantastic episode of Remedios the Beauty's ascent heavenward, with its possible religious implications, is brought to a close by the statement that there might have been talk of nothing else for a long time if the barbarous extermination of the Aurelianos had not replaced amazement with horror. The writer then proceeds to relate a series of senseless brutalities culminating with the murders of sixteen of the seventeen sons of Colonel Aureliano Buendía, all on the same night.

In addition to the stylistic and structural elements discussed above, *One Hundred Years of Solitude* abounds in symbolic images, parallel constructions, and other poetic devices contributing to its lyrical nature, overflowing vitality, and compositional unity. Several important aspects of this vast fictional universe are suggested in the opening lines, namely its genesis ("The world was so recent that many things lacked names"); its potential development ("Macondo was a village of twenty adobe houses, built on the bank of a river of clear water that ran along a bed of polished stones, which were white and enormous, like prehistoric eggs"); and its tragic and symbolic elements ("Many years later, as he faced the firing squad, Colonel Aureliano Buendía was to remember that distant afternoon when his father took him to discover ice").

Ice is to become one of the most important motifs, illuminating the thematic trajectory from the utopian idea of progress to frustration, disillusionment, death, and destruction. As soon as José Arcadio Buendía discovers ice he relates it to his dream of a city with mirror-walled houses and resolves to build dwellings with the marvelous material. Later Melquíades reads in a book of prophesies by the sixteenth-century astrologer Nostradamus that Macondo will become a great city of luminous glass houses, but José Arcadio Buendía insists they will be made of ice. The old patriarch's utopian dreams are subsequently shattered, however, by his confrontation with death in a labyrinth of identical rooms, an ironic reconstuction of his initial vision of Macondo.

When the enterprising Aureliano Triste (one of Colonel Aureliano Buendía's seventeen illegitimate sons) brings the train to Macondo in order to expand his ice business to the neighboring communities, ice emerges as an instrument of progress. But the train also brings gringo imperialism and, along with it, the seeds of the town's eventual ruin. A related idea is suggested in the final lines of the book when the destruction of the "city of mirrors or mirages)" evokes the ephemeral nature of ice as well as the dreams it symbolizes for José Arcadio Buendía.

Another leitmotif that parallels the plot's development and reinforces thematic content is the enchanted region near Macondo, a fabulous, prehistoric forest first mentioned when José Arcadio Buendía sets out to find "civilization." After wandering through this "paradise" for a week, he and his men are suddenly confronted by an enormous Spanish galleon adorned with orchids and exuding an air of "solitude and oblivion." Many years later it is rumored that the gringos are planting banana groves in this area, and when Fernanda takes her daughter Meme to a convent in the interior, the train passes by the "carbonized skeleton of the Spanish galleon," the gringos' neat, white houses equipped with fans, and the wretched lodgings built for the workers. Subsequently Amaranta Ursula's husband, Gaston, builds a landing strip in the enchanted region, hoping to pioneer Macondo's first airmail service. And in the last reference to the area in question, we are informed that perhaps Patricia Brown has told her grandchildren in Prattville, Alabama about the far-off banana-company town, now a "plain of wild grass."

An important aspect of the lyrical novel that also characterizes *One Hundred Years of Solitude* is its dependence on poetic images to heighten aesthetic pleasure. These images frequently blend with the characters, revealing their essential traits and fixing them more firmly in the mind of the reader. Thus the giant chestnut tree to which José Arcadio Buendía is tied reflects the immense size and strength of the patriarchal figure. The smell of smoke emanating from Pilar Ternera indicates the sexual passion still smoldering within her aging body. The black gauze bandage worn by Amaranta on the hand she thrusts into the fire after Pietro Crespi's suicide symbolizes both her virginity and the sterility of her existence. Colonel Aureliano Buendías solitude is underscored by the painful sores in his armpits as well as by the chills from which he suffers almost constantly throughout the latter part of his life. And the swarms of yellow butterflies hovering around Mauricio Babilonia represent his animal magnetism for Meme, but for Fernanda they signify bad luck and thus foreshadow the tragic end of his affair with Meme.

García Márquez's sensuous style and unusual figures of speech constitute additional sources of the novel's volcanic vitality. The frequent confusion of the concrete and the abstract heightens psychic tension and emotional impact by creating ambiguity and jarring the reader onto new levels of awareness. Examples are numerous. Aureliano Buendía has been carrying his desire for Pilar Ternera since infancy in an "inviolable backwater of his heart." The rain fills Aureliano Segundo "with the spongy serenity of a lack of appetite." To ease her frustrations caused by the absence of Pietro Crespi, Rebeca eats handfuls of dirt leaving "a harsh aftertaste in her mouth and a sediment of peace in her heart." In a futile attempt to break "the hard shell of his solitude," Colonel Aureliano Buendía scratches for hours on end. Meme senses herself "splashing in the bog of hesitation" before stumbling into an "open space of lucidity." In bed with his Aunt Amaranta, Aureliano José feels the hand without the black bandage "diving like a blind shellfish into the algae of his anxiety." Aureliano Segundo becomes lost "in labyrinths of disappointment" while seeking Fernanda. Melquíades speaks, "lighting up with his deep organ voice the darkest reaches of the imagination." And José Arcadio Buendía sees "a route that could only lead to the past."

Dramatic emphasis and ambiguity are also rendered by the use of oxymoron, i.e., the concomitant use of incongruous or contradictory words. Thus in her affair with Mauricio Babilonia, Meme is protected by the "innocent complicity" of her father, Aureliano Segundo. When José Arcadio steals into Pilar Ternera's room at night, the door hinges yield with an "articulate moan." Upon surrendering to José Arcadio's caresses, Rebeca loses herself in the "inconceivable pleasure of that unbearable pain." José Arcadio bursts forth with an outpouring of "tender obscenities" while making love to the gypsy girl. Sexual passions tend to take on cosmic dimensions resulting in comic effect as demonstrated in the following phrases. The prostitute Nigromanta "found a man [Aureliano Babilonia] whose tremendous power demanded a movement of seismic readjustment from her insides." "A great commotion immobilized her [Amaranta Ursula] in her center of gravity." ". . . a startlingly regulated cyclonic power lifted her [Rebeca] up by the waist and despoiled her of her intimacy." And José Arcadio "could no longer resist the glacial rumbling of his kidneys."

Hyperbole is not always an element of comedy, however, as demonstrated in the following description of the army's entrance into Macondo to bring an end to the strike:

There were three regiments, whose march in time to a drum made the earth tremble. Their snorting of a many-headed dragon filled the glow of noon with a pestilential vapor. They were short, stocky, and brutelike. They perspired with the sweat of a horse and emitted an odor of suntanned hide and the taciturn and impenetrable perseverence of men from the highlands. Although it took them more than an hour to pass by, one might have thought that they were only a few squads marching in a circle, because they were all identical, sons of the same bitch, and with the same stolidity they all bore the weight of their packs and canteens, the shame of their rifles with fixed bayonets, and the chancre of blind obedience and a sense of honor.

The above passage contains an abundance of sharply contrasting, sensorial images and concepts. An initial impression of fantastic power is rendered by the trembling earth and the comparison of the troops with a many-headed dragon. Their short stature and animal nature, however, are earthy, naturalistic details that acquire an absurd, hypnotic quality as a result of their identical appearance and the illusion that they are "marching in a circle." Finally, the juxtaposition of their physical and moral discomfort ("the weight of their packs and canteens, the shame of their rifles with fixed bayonets") and the paradoxical nature of their values ("the chancre of blind obedience and a sense of honor") create the kind of tension, tonal modulation, and ambiguity that are maintained throughout the narration of the strike.

Like many of today's writers, García Márquez reveals a strong nostalgia for the past that has been buried under a sterile, chromium civilization presently in a state of irreversible decay. Man's loss of innocence in a universe from which God has withdrawn has brought about his detachment from nature as well as the severance of his intimate relations with his fellow men. The result is the kind of cosmic homelessness reflected in the characters' solitude, a recurring motif and the novel's principal theme. Although García Márquez depicts the perennial forces of irrationality, injustice, degradation, and violence that plague human existence, he at the same time soothes and enchants the reader with countercurrents of pathos, poetic fantasy, and hyperbolic humor, often soaring to contrapuntal heights rarely achieved in contemporary literature. Indeed, he has few peers in breathing movement and laughter into a tale. The disproportion between the characters' intentions and the adverse reality they face illuminates the futility of their struggles for self-fulfillment and lays the groundwork for the absurdities and baffling inconsistencies that occupy a central position in their lives.

Time constitutes a second major theme, the terror and solitude engendered by rational thought and lineal history being partially alleviated by myth and the pervasive patterns of cyclical renewal. However, the crushing weight of the past ultimately brings temporal progress to a standstill and the novel to its tragic end. There clearly emerges an indictment of the stifling impulses of the modern age and of the insidious mechanisms by which society creates its victims. The sole solution, it would seem, lies in the love, integrity, and human solidarity demonstrated by a few of the characters, such as Ursula, Aureliano Segundo, and Petra Cotes.

One Hundred Years of Solitude synthesizes virtually all levels of human reality including the historic and mythical, the individual and collective, the tragic and humorous, and the logical and fantastic. Its structural configuration consists of a spiral of concentric circles representing a family, a town, a nation, a continent, and all mankind. The novel's mythical underpinnings, moreover, reinforce the formal design, enhancing artistic unity and granting universal significance to the everyday experience. Whether it is read as an historically allusive family chronicle or as a metaphor of all human endeavor, it is likely to revive experiences for all those who have been enchanted by *The Arabian Nights*, laughed with Cervantes and Rabelais, or become immersed in Faulkner's imaginary Yoknapatawpha County. García Márquez has combined a variety of old and new literary devices to expand the limits of fictional reality and restore plot to its central position in the art of story telling. His finished product is a work of extraordinary density, dramatic tension, and ironic resonance. Nor can one overlook the seductive powers of language that stimulates the imagination with symbolic nuances and captivating sensorial imagery.

García Márquez has asserted that his masterpiece is completely lacking in seriousness, that he only intended to tell the story of a family that lived in terror of incest and made every effort to avoid begetting a child with a pig's tail. A somewhat similar attitude is expressed by Aureliano Babilonia in the final pages of the novel when he discovers literature to be the best plaything ever invented for making fun of people. *One Hundred Years of Solitude* will nevertheless impress many readers, not only as a commentary of profound concern for the terrible realities of the human condition, but also as a haunting premonition of disaster. Ultimately, however, it is a monumental tour de force by a nonpareil spinner of yarns whose somber vision of a disintegrating world is surpassed only by his sense of humor and artistic excellence.[5]

5

~~~~~~

Fantasy Prevails

In 1972, García Márquez published *The Incredible and Sad Tale of Innocent Eréndira and Her Heartless Grandmother*, a volume of seven short stories.[1] Although Macondo has disappeared as the setting for these tales, some of the characters and literary techniques have a familiar ring to devotees of García Márquez's previous works. The title story is by far the longest of the collection and one of the more realistic, its principal themes being human exploitation and revenge. The protagonist, Eréndira, is a placid fourteen-year-old girl living with her grandmother in a mansion located in an isolated desert community. The grotesquely obese grandmother, referred to on several occasions as the "white whale," is the widow of a former smuggler named Amadís, who, it is rumored, had brought her to her present home from a brothel on one of the Caribbean islands. When her husband and son died, the grandmother dismissed all the servants, retaining only the docile Eréndira to perform the innumerable household tasks. One night after the exhausted child falls asleep, her "wind of misfortune" tips over the candle next to her bed and the mansion is reduced to ashes. Thus Eréndira is obliged to recoup her grandmother's lost fortune by turning to prostitution. Within a short time after the fire the resounding success of their enterprise enables them to purchase a burro and set out for greener pastures with a retinue of Indian porters, musicians, and a photographer.

During their travels Eréndira meets a naive youth named Ulises whose Dutch father makes his living by raising diamond-centered oranges and smuggling them across the border. A short time later Eréndira is kidnaped and taken to a mission run by Spanish friars where she is obliged to whitewash stairsteps until she is "liberated" by her grandmother. The old lady also manages to secure a letter from a corrupt politician, Senator Onésimo Sánchez, who vouches for her (the old lady's) high moral character and thus enhances her granddaughter's growing professional reputation. Meanwhile, Ulises, having fallen in love with Eréndira, escapes from his parents' farm in their station wagon and persuades the girl to run away with him. The two are overtaken by the police after a wild chase and returned to their respective guardians.

From this time on, Eréndira remains chained to her bed. Her grandmother converts their steadily increasing wealth into gold bars, which she keeps in a sailcloth vest she wears virtually all the time. Soon after they arrive at the seashore, the old lady makes the mistake of telling Eréndira that some day, when her grandmother is gone, she will be rich, happy, and free. Eréndira then summons Ulises "with all the strength of her interior voice" and induces him to murder her exploiter. The story ends with the grandmother's violent death and the girl's solitary flight.

Like most of García Márquez's works, "Innocent Eréndira" is based on actual conditions in his native land. The setting of the story is the Guajira Peninsula, an arid region bordering on Venezuela where smuggling is an all-too-common enterprise. The power of the church emerges when the local authorities refuse to help the grandmother put pressure on the mission to release Eréndira because according to the concordat (an agreement between the papacy and the government) the monks have the right to keep the girl as long as she is an unmarried minor. Moreover, with the aid of military detachments, the "men of God" scour the countryside in search of single pregnant women, obliging them to marry their lovers in spite of their objections that wives are treated much worse than concubines. The end of the tale takes place near an unnamed port city from which Eréndira's grandmother has intended to sail for Aruba, an island located off the northwest coast of Venezuela.

The fact that "Innocent Eréndira" was originally written as a film script probably explains its heavy reliance on visual imagery and dramatic scene for its fundamental narrative techniques. Thus, like a roving camera eye the objective narrator depends exclusively on physical description, action, and dialogue to delineate his characters, whose inner lives remain unrevealed, increasing the aesthetic distance between them and the reader and limiting the reader's emotional involvement.

In marked contrast to the story's tragically realistic underpinnings are its occasional flights of fantasy and bursts of humor stemming from overstatement, paradox, and the grotesque, all told with a straight face. For example, the love-smitten Ulises's state of mind manifests itself when all the glass objects he touches turn different colors. It takes Eréndira two hours to bathe and dress her grandmother and six hours to wind the clocks in their "enormous mansion of moonlike concrete." Ulises is described as a "gilded adolescent with lonely, maritime eyes and the look of a furtive angel." Nevertheless, he makes two attempts on the grandmother's life before he finally murders her with a carving knife. The mission in which Eréndira is held captive is not dedicated to the struggle

against the devil, but rather against the hostile desert
environment where the mere physical survival of the
mission inhabitants hangs in the balance. Thus, incredible tasks are assigned to the nuns, one of whom
chases a pig through the patio, catches it by the ears,
and wallows with it in a mudhole "until two novices
with leather aprons helped her hold it down and one
of them cut its throat with a butcher knife and they
all remained soaked in blood and mud."

The grotesque mixture of farce and horror also
characterizes Ulises's unsuccessful attempts to kill
Eréndira's grandmother. On the first occasion he bakes
her a birthday cake containing enough arsenic to kill
"a generation of rats," and her only visible reaction
after devouring it at one sitting is the loss of her hair,
which she delightedly pulls out and replaces with a
"wig of radiant feathers." He then puts dynamite in
the piano and ignites the fuse while the old lady is
playing it, but once more she emerges almost un-
scathed. When he finally stabs her, her blood is "oily,
shiny, and green."

The story's texture is also enriched by the inclusion of symbolic imagery and literary and mythical
allusions. The sensuous language of the opening pages
describing the grandmother's mansion parodies the
style utilized by the Latin-American modernists prior
to World War I.[2] Eréndira's "wind of misfortune"
emerges as a leitmotif, first foreshadowing and then
underscoring her tragic existence, and the "white
whale" (her grandmother), as a symbol of evil reminiscent of Melville's Moby Dick. Ironically, Ulises
never attains the heroic stature of his Greek mythical
namesake, but remains a bumbling fool until the end
of the story when he is seen lying face down on the
beach, "weeping from solitude and fear." Ironic contrast also characterizes the grandmother's smuggler
husband Amadís and his legendary counterpart Ama-

dís de Gaula, the brave and virtuous protagonist of a famous sixteenth-century Spanish novel of chivalry by the same name.

The image of the sea in the final pages of the tale emerges as a possible symbol of destruction and cyclical renewal, meanings often conveyed by this archetypal motif. So long as they are in the desert the obedient Eréndira shows no sign whatsoever of revolt against her cruel grandmother, but soon after their arrival at the seashore, she induces Ulises to perform his nefarious deed. And once his mission has been accomplished, Eréndira disappears clutching her gold-filled vest and abandoning her exhausted lover. Her ruthless exploitation of Ulises and her subsequent display of avarice suggest the possibility that she represents the rebirth of the recently murdered "white whale." If this is indeed the case, the archetypal image of the sea serves to illuminate the mythical cycle of death and regeneration. However, the fact that regeneration occurs without the usual intervening process of purification implies a pessimistic assessment of the human endeavor.

The story's pervasive tone of irony derives from several factors. The lengthy mock-epic title, with its suggestion of unforgettable deeds, is likely to elicit a quizzical smile from the prospective reader. The detached narrator's point of view limits the reader's feelings of identification with the characters, making him in effect an ironic observer of their absurd escapades. An ironic response is also generated by the use of hyperbole and paradox as well as by the sharp discrepancy between the events themselves and the serious manner in which they are told. Moreover, the plot would seem to represent an inversion of the traditional fairy tale in which the mythical hero slays the terrible dragon (the grandmother) in order to free the innocent damsel in distress and found his own kingdom.

This ironic reversal is reinforced by the name Eréndira, a word closely resembling the Spanish verb
rendir meaning *to conquer*, which is precisely what
the protagonist manages to do.

Perhaps the most noticeable defect of this tragicomic tale manifests itself toward the end when a
first-person narrator unexpectedly identifies himself as
a footloose encyclopedia salesman and renders a brief
description of the circus-like atmosphere surrounding
Eréndira and her picturesque retinue. This abrupt
shift in the point of view, from that of a neutral outside observer to that of an inside and probably unreliable raconteur, injects into the work a note of
incongruity difficult to justify either thematically or
aesthetically. "Innocent Eréndira" also suffers from a
kind of coldness at its inner core, its mixture of farce
and objectivity leaving the reader more amused than
moved by the adverse fate of the characters. Still, its
rapid movement and adroit fusion of fantasy and
reality make it difficult not to finish this long story at
one sitting.

"The Sea of Lost Time" is one of the two weakest
pieces and the only one written before *One Hundred
Years of Solitude*. The setting is a dying pueblo located
next to the sea, which is generally regarded as a cruel,
destructive force in the lives of the people. One night
the almost totally unknown fragrance of roses, apparently carried aloft by the seaward winds, permeates
the atmosphere of the town. Petra, the aging wife of
Jacob, is tired of living and perceives the phenomenon
as a sign of her approaching death. Shortly thereafter
she dies. When the same pleasant odor returns, Tobías
is the first to notice it and excitedly informs his skeptical wife, Clotilde, as well as the rest of the inhabitants. Soon the smell of roses becomes so strong that
it attracts large numbers of outsiders who fill the streets
and create a kind of carnival atmosphere in the com-

munity. Even a priest arrives declaring that God has chosen to favor them with his blessing. About this time a fabulously wealth gringo named Mr. Herbert also appears and announces his intention to distribute money to the needy. Instead, he proceeds to exploit them as seen in the case of the game of checkers he plays blindfolded with Jacob, winning all the old man's possessions. Mr. Herbert also arranges a week-long fiesta during which he displays an ingeniously drawn sketch of a city with immense glass buildings supposedly representing the town's brilliant future. After the celebration, however, he sleeps for "days on end." Meanwhile, the smell of roses disappears and the pleasure-seeking newcomers abandon the pueblo, which returns to its previous state of decay. The priest forgets his plans to build a temple and, convinced that the town has fallen into mortal sin and that the fragrance will never return, packs his suitcases and leaves with the money he has collected for the new church. When Mr. Herbert finally awakens and views the devastation, he invites the imaginative Tobías to accompany him on a turtle hunt to the bottom of the sea where, after a series of fantastic adventures among both the living and the dead, they return to the village. The tale ends with Mr. Herbert's departure and Tobías's vain attempt to relate the details of his journey to his wife.

Although "The Sea of Lost Time" stands out as one of García Márquez's least interesting tales, it is important in the evolution of his fictional universe because its structural design anticipates that of his masterpiece five years later. For example, the fragrance emanating from the sea emerges as a symbol of hope analogous to José Arcadio Buendía's dream of a city of mirror-walled houses just prior to his founding of Macondo. Moreover, the town's burst of prosperity and ensuing decline, as well as the key roles played therein by Mr. Herbert and adverse tropical nature, foreshadow a similar chain of events determining the fate of Macondo. The injection of fantasy characterizing "The Sea of Lost Time" is destined to become one of the hallmarks of virtually all García Márquez's subsequent writings. And the symbolic role of hope in the tale implies that without this important ingredient in human existence, man and his society are condemned to languish.

Another story of lesser significance is "Death Constant Beyond Love," which concerns an ailing politician's confrontation with death. The forty-two-year-old Senator Onésimo Sánchez has just learned that he has six months to live when he arrives at a poverty-stricken seaside community during his reelection campaign. His pompous, promise-filled speech, which is accompanied by frayed cardboard backdrops presumably representing the town's future progress, is followed by his frank declaration before a small group of civic leaders that it is to their advantage to reelect him in order to maintain the status quo and preserve their privileges. Another, more human aspect of Sánchez's character is suggested by a rose he has brought with him to the arid community and a paper butterfly he fashions from a calendar while making one of his speeches. When he throws the butterfly into the current of air from a ventilator, it is carried to a wall where it becomes permanently embedded in the plaster, as if it were a painting. The story is brought to its climax when an ex-convict seeking a favor sends his beautiful daughter, Laura, to spend the night with Sánchez. The senator's lust wanes because of his overwhelming fear and loneliness, but the girl's beauty and innocence make him realize that he has found the "woman of his life." Though obscure in meaning, "Death Constant Beyond Love" seems to be concerned with the complexities of human behavior in the face

of death. The protagonist's cynicism continues unabated for a time, as indicated by his hyprocritical
speeches and the cardboard backdrops, reflections of
his empty promises of material progress. By way of
contrast, the rose and the butterfly embedded in the
wall suggest his appreciation of beauty and innocence.
In the final lines of the story his love for Laura becomes his only weapon against metaphysical anguish.
It would seem to signify a triumph of perennial human values over crass political ambitions.

"A Very Old Man with Enormous Wings" and
"The Handsomest Drowned Man in the World" are
two of García Márquez's most charming stories, both
having been written for children. Despite the similarities of their settings and structural designs, these two
works present opposite themes: the former depicts a
lonely, decaying world, while the latter conveys a
more optimistic assessment of man's potential. "A Very
Old Man with Enormous Wings" has its setting in a
poor village by the sea. One gray, stormy day Pelayo,
disposing of the crabs that have accumulated in his
courtyard, discovers an old man with wings lying face
down in the mud. Pelayo and his wife, Elisenda, carefully examine the bald, almost toothless creature who is
dressed like a ragpicker. When he answers their inquiries in an unknown tongue, they conclude he must
be a castaway from a foreign ship wrecked by the
storm or perhaps, as their imaginative neighbor suggests, a fugitive from a celestial conspiracy. After en-
closing him in the chicken coop for the night, they
decide to set him adrift on a raft the following day.
However, the next morning crowds of people appear
to view the "flesh-and-blood angel," whom they pro-
ceed to treat as if he were some sort of circus animal.
They also make all kinds of suggestions concerning
what should be done with him, some thinking he

should be named mayor of the world, others that he should be made a five-star general, and still others that he should be put to stud in order to create a race of winged wise men. It occurs to Elisenda to charge a five-cent admission fee to look at him. Soon thereafter a line of eagerly waiting spectators extends from the couple's courtyard to the horizon. The old man with wings, however, remains coldly indifferent to the curiosity seekers.

Meanwhile the priest, Father Gonzaga, examines the newcomer and concludes that because he does not understand Latin, God's language, he could be an instrument of the devil. For this reason a letter is sent off to the bishop with the request that a verdict on the issue be solicited through the chain of command up to the Supreme Pontiff. Instead of dealing with the priest's questions, however, the communications from Rome inquire if the angel has a navel and if he could possibly be a Norwegian with wings. When invalids come to the village in search of miraculous cures through contact with the heavenly creature, the results are disappointing. For example, a blind man grows three new teeth, a paralytic almost wins the lottery, and a leper's sores sprout sunflowers. Thus people begin to lose interest in the aging captive and, instead, direct their attention toward a road show featuring a woman who has been transformed into a tarantula for disobeying her parents. During this time Pelayo has made use of his newly acquired wealth to build a luxurious, two-story house with iron bars on the windows "to keep out crabs and angels," while Elisenda buys a pair of satin pumps and some iridescent silk dresses like those worn by the most stylish women of the community. Soon thereafter both the couple's child and the angel come down with chicken pox, and the doctor summoned to treat them cannot resist the temptation to examine the angel's wings, the formation of which he finds so natural that he cannot understand why all men do not grow them.

Eventually the chicken coop collapses because of the rain, and the aging creature makes his way into the house where his inopportune appearances elicit exclamations of displeasure from Elisenda ("It was awful living in that hell full of angels.") One morning while she is chopping onions she catches sight of him in the courtyard flapping his wings like a "senile vulture" in an attempt to fly away. As he gains altitude and disappears in the distance, she sighs with relief because "then he was no longer an annoyance in her life but an imaginary dot on the horizon of the sea."

"A Very Old Man with Enormous Wings" is particularly intriguing because it can be read on several different levels. First of all it is a delightful fantasy for children. For the adult reader, however, the protagonist reinforces themes pervading many of García Márquez's works: the angel's decrepitude is another example of physical decay; man's loss of innocence is suggested by the angel's fall from his heavenly abode to an unhappy earthly existence; the failure of the church is conveyed by the preposterous ecclesiastical investigation of the angel; and the theme of solitude emerges from the angel's uncommunicative nature and isolation from all men. The absurd attempts to explain the angel's appearance logically and to discover his *raison d'être* demonstrate the limits of human reason, whereas his reduction to the status of a sideshow freak for the monetary gain of others implies a condemnation of capitalistic exploitation. On a mythical level, the angel recalls the youthful Greek hero Icarus who defied the gods by flying too close to the sun, melting the wax by which his wings were attached and causing him to plummet into the sea. The old man, however, suggests an ironic reversal of the Greek myth, a symbol of modern alienation and decadence, that contrasts sharply with a more poetic and heroic past.

The protagonist's disappearance at the end of the story is fraught with ambiguity. On the one hand, Elisenda's sigh of relief at having him out of sight suggests, pessimistically, the extinction in today's world of brotherly love and solidarity among men. On the other hand, the fact that he manages to take flight and fade into the "horizon of the sea" could signify the cathartic destruction of antiquated myths and thus a prelude to the rebirth of human values.

Purification and rebirth clearly emerge as major themes of "The Handsomest Drowned Man in the World," the action of which also takes place in a drab seaside village. One day the corpse of an unknown man weighing "almost as much as a horse" is washed ashore where children are playing. With great difficulty he is carried to a nearby house while the men of the town set out for the neighboring communities to inquire if anyone is missing. Meanwhile the women preparing the dead man for burial discover him to be so tall, strong, and virile that "there was not enough room for him in their imagination." Because their husbands' clothes are much too small for him, they sew a pair of trousers and a shirt to enable him to "continue through death with dignity." While gazing at him in fascination, they imagine how powerful, commanding, and superior to other men he must have been during his lifetime. However, after they have christened him Esteban, he assumes more human proportions, appearing awkward because of his enormous size and apologetic for the inconvenience he is causing them. Indeed, the women are so moved by his air of sincerity and destitution that they burst into uncontrollable sobs. But when their husbands return with the news that the deceased is unknown in the region, the mourners cease to weep and jubilantly proclaim him to be theirs.

Esteban's funeral is attended by crowds of people
bearing flowers from neighboring villages. In order
that he will not be buried as an orphan, the leading
citizens are designated as members of his family, creating the impression that "through him all the inhabitants of the village became kinsmen." During the ceremony, as they gaze at the "splendor and beauty" of
the dead man, the townspeople become aware for the
first time of the desolation of their streets and the
barrenness of their lives. At the same time they are
convinced that because of Esteban their lives will
undergo a change for the better. Houses will be built
with wider doors, higher ceilings, and stronger floors
to keep his memory alive. Flowers will be cultivated
on the rocky cliffs so that travelers on passing steamers
will awaken, "suffocated by the smell of gardens on
the high seas." And sea captains will point to the
promontory of roses on the horizon and exclaim in
fourteen languages, "That's Esteban's village." "The
Handsomest Drowned Man in the World" is reminiscent of the myth of Prometheus, the Greek hero who
gave fire to mankind. Esteban's gifts, however, are
beauty, hope and human solidarity, the keys to happiness and the best antidotes for human degradation.

"Blancamán the Good, Vendor of Miracles" and
"The Last Voyage of the Ghost Ship" are the two
stories of this collection that most clearly indicate new
trends in García Márquez's fiction since the publication of *One Hundred Years of Solitude*. Blancamán
the Good is a *pícaro* who describes his fantastic and
highly amusing adventures with his cruel, charlatan
employer, Blancamán the Bad. The young narrator
first sees his future exploiter when, standing before a
captive audience, Blancamán the Bad "proves" the
efficacy of his antidote for snakebite by allowing a
bushmaster to bite him, and after "fainting" and rolling about on the ground for a few minutes, pretends

to regain consciousness. While hawking their patent medicines along the Caribbean coast, the two find themselves in dire financial straits for which Blancamán the Bad blames his assistant and subjects him to sadistic punishment. Blancamán the Good suddenly finds himself endowed with magical powers when he seizes a dead rabbit from his tormentor's hand, hurls it against a wall, and it comes back to life. He leaves his master and soon achieves renown as a healer of the infirm, undertaking any feat except that of reviving the dead because they are likely to become enraged at being disturbed and either commit suicide or die of disillusionment. Eventually he acquires an automobile, a chauffeur, and a chain of businesses where medals of his profile are sold to tourists. Toward the end of the story Blancamán the Bad reappears, now old, ill, and professing repentance for his past sins. He dies before a crowd of spectators while attempting to demonstrate his supernatural powers by eating a can of *barbasco* roots, and although Blancamán the Good is present during the entire spectacle, he is unable—or more than likely unwilling—to save him. Blancamán the Good has a requiem mass sung for the deceased by three bishops, builds a mausoleum for his remains on a bluff overlooking the sea, and then takes revenge on his torturer by resuscitating him and leaving him to weep in his tomb for eternity.

As demonstrated by the preceding summary, humor and fantasy, often derived from the use of hyperbole, assume even greater proportions in this story than in the others, the accumulation of absurdities serving to accelerate and intensify the narrative tempo. Additional examples are numerous. While Blancamán the Bad is supposedly dying after having been bitten by the bushmaster, an American cruiser that has been docked nearby on a goodwill mission for twenty years declares a quarantine to prevent the snake poison from getting on board. Furthermore, when the American marines begin to take colored photographs of the "dying" man with long-distance lenses, a group of women on their way home from church hasten to cover him with a blanket to protect his body from profanation by the "Adventist instruments" (a reference to Seventh-Day-Adventist missionaries in the country). Having witnessed Blancamán the Bad's successful demonstration of the antidote, the admiral of the cruiser buys a bottle of the patent medicine, convinced that it would be useful against "poisoned anarchist bullets." Some time later in Philadelphia he repeats the charlatan's experiment with a venomous snake and is transformed into a "glob of admiral jelly in front of his staff." This incident and an epidemic of yellow fever serve as pretexts for an invasion of the country by Yankee marines. Their numerous atrocities include chopping off the heads of Chinese for distraction, of Negroes from habit, and of Hindus because they are snake charmers.

In his days of glory, Blancamán the Bad had been an extraordinarily successful embalmer of viceroys, having given their faces such authority that they governed posthumously for many years better than they did when they were alive. He also extracted molars by suggestion, peddled "escape suppositories" to make smugglers transparent, and sold "furtive drops" for baptized wives to dissolve in soup in order to instill the fear of God in Dutch husbands. He was even capable of convincing an astronomer that the month of February was nothing but a herd of invisible elephants. His sadistic torture of Blancamán the Good takes several ingenious forms. After beating the youth mercilessly, he discovers a "practical application for the electricity of suffering" by inventing a sewing machine he delightedly operates with the aid of cupping glasses attached to the most bruised parts of his victim's body. He also rolls his assistant up in barbed wire, rubs salt into his sores, hangs him up by the ankles in the blistering sun, and finally throws him into the penance dungeon of an abandoned mission where he tantalizes him by imitating the "voices of edible animals" and "the noise of ripe beets."

The story's atmosphere of magic and caprice is underscored by its temporal contradictions and distortions. For example, Blancamán the Good's automobile and the marines' cameras with color film and telephoto lenses would logically place the action in the twentieth century, but the use of coins such as the *real*, the *cuartillo*, and the *doubloon* constitutes on oblique allusion to the Spanish colonial period. The question of time enters the realm of fantasy when Blancamán the Good states that his first encounter with Blancamán the Bad occurred "more than a century ago" and, in the final lines, that Blancamán the Bad "will keep on living in his tomb as long as I'm alive, that is, forever."

Still, the most notable innovations in "Blancamán the Good, Vendor of Miracles" are not to be found in its content, but rather in its rambling, digressive style, which often compresses abrupt temporal dislocations and shifting points of view into a single sentence. In the following example Blancamán the Good's third-person, past-tense description of the last time he saw Blancamán the Bad alive is ingeniously fused with Blancamán the Bad's plaintive confession, in first person and present tense, before a crowd of spellbound spectators:

"The last time anyone saw him in this world he'd lost even the studs of his former splendor, and his soul was a shambles and his bones in disorder from the rigors of the desert, but he still had enough spunk left to reappear that Sunday in Santa María del Darién with his eternal sepulchral trunk, except that on that occasion he wasn't

trying to sell an antidote, but was asking in a voice
cracked with emotion that the marines shoot him in a public
spectacle so that he could demonstrate on his own flesh
the life-restoring properties of this supernatural creature,
ladies and gentlemen, and although you certainly have
cause not to believe me after suffering so long from my
evil tricks as a liar and a faker, I swear on the bones of my
mother that this proof today is nothing from the other
world, but rather the humble truth, and in case you have
any doubts left, be assured that I'm not laughing now
the way I used to, but holding back a desire to cry."

"The Last Voyage of the Ghost Ship" is unique
among García Márquez's pieces of short fiction, for
in addition to its sudden changes in narrative perspective and excursive style—the entire story consists of a
single sentence—it describes a kind of surrealistic
dream in which the mentally disturbed protagonist
gives vent to his erratic urges for power and revenge.
He first catches sight of the enormous, silent ocean
liner one night when, still a boy, he gazes from the
seaside village where he lives toward the colonial port
city on the other side of the bay. The boat, which disappears when a flashing beacon strikes its side and
becomes visible again when the light has passed, suddenly veers toward dangerous, invisible shoals, runs
aground, and sinks without making a sound. The next
day the boy is convinced it was all a nightmare because everything seems to be normal. However, the
following March, exactly a year later, he has a similar
vision that he recounts to his widowed mother. Soon
thereafter she dies, leaving her son penniless and
utterly alone in a community that is hostile to him
because of the mysterious circumstances surrounding
her death and that of several other women. The next
time the huge liner appears, the excited youth awakens
the town's inhabitants and is soundly beaten for the
disturbance he has caused. He rages against his assail-

ants, repeating to himself over and over again a phrase destined to become a leitmotif, "Now they are going to see who I am." The following March he steals a rowboat, crosses the bay, and waits for the giant vessel to return. When he finally catches sight of it noiselessly heading toward the shoals, he lights the tiny red lantern on his boat and proceeds to guide it into the main channel toward the docks of the seaport nearby. Moments later, however, the ghost ship suddenly comes to life, resembling a typical transatlantic steamer, and the youth, still carrying his "leftover rage" and repeating "Now they are going to see who I am, the cowards," abruptly changes his course and directs the liner toward the lights of his village. He barely has time to get out of the way before the colossal product of his imagination, "twenty times taller than the church steeple and some ninety-seven times longer than the pueblo," comes crashing ashore before the eyes of the astonished townspeople.

The surrealistic seascape of "The Last Voyage of the Ghost Ship" abounds in sharply delineated, dreamlike images strongly indicative of the protagonist's schizophrenic tendencies, i.e., his constant vacillation between the poles of confidence or hostile self-assertion and disillusionment or self-annihilation. His split personality is first suggested in the opening lines when the flashing beacon alternately focuses on the village, which it transforms into "a lunar encampment of glowing houses," and then on the dark, silent ocean liner that drifts toward the shoals and disappears. Subsequently, the boy's unstable perceptions of reality oscillate between the luminous beauty of frolicking tropical fish such as manta rays, pink porgies, and blue corvinas, on the one hand, and the stench of rotten salamanders, on the other. In the last episode his aggressive impulses are conveyed by the roar of his voice, and his tendency toward withdrawal, by the

eerie image of him rowing toward the harbor under
the flashing beacon, "so wrapped up in himself that
he did not know why the night became so dense, as
if the stars had died." Suddenly the gigantic vessel
looms forth, "darker than any other thing on land or
sea, three hundred thousand tons of shark odor . . .
carrying its own circle of silence, its own dead air, its
halted time." Moments later, however, it comes to life,
illuminated by bright lights, exuding exotic smells, and
throbbing with musical sounds. The description of its
cataclysmic destruction, brought about by the young
man's "leftover rage" and intense longing to assert his
power over his "enemies," climaxes and ends with the
specter of the wrecked hull dripping "ancient and
languid waters of the seas of death" down its sides.

"The Last Voyage of the Ghost Ship" is a phantasmagorical exploration of an unstable psyche whose
fleeting visions, set forth in highly stylized, contrasting
patterns, make this one of its author's most original
and compelling pieces of short fiction.

Although García Márquez's most recent tales
never match the perfection of *One Hundred Years of
Solitude*, several do reconfirm his ability as a consummate literary craftsman. Aesthetic unity is achieved
by the recurring themes and settings of the stories,
which, altogether, depict the solitude, physical and
spiritual decay, and human suffering characteristic of
life in the isolated Atlantic coastal region of Colombia.
The heavy reliance on sensorial images serves not only
as a means to communicate plot and fluctuating moods,
but also as a structural device to delineate archetypal
patterns of disintegration and renewal. Indeed, the
spectacle of social decadence momentarily alleviated
by the mirage of material progress appears to be one
of García Márquez's major thematic obsessions.

Despite the allusions to the writer's native land,
fantasy emerges as the collection's dominant element,

ranging from the mysterious phenomena affecting entire communities to the inner, surrealistic visions of
sensitive or deranged individuals. These magical aspects of subjective reality enhance the barren lives of
the characters and contribute to the creation of a total,
self-contained fictional world in which imagination
outweighs the laws of logic. Literary dimensions are
also expanded by frequent bursts of grotesque humor
as well as by temporal dislocations and deftly manipulated shifts in the narrative perspective. Thus, whereas
the effaced-narrator technique of the title story renders
the direct, visual quality of a movie projector, the author's limited omniscience in "The Last Voyage of the
Ghost Ship" narrows the focus to the irrational protagonist's point of view, and the rambling, first-person
narrative voice of "Blancamán the Good, Vendor of
Miracles" conveys the close-up immediacy and irony
of the unreliable narrator that typify this method of
telling a tale.

Inasmuch as García Márquez's stories often parody rather than depict the world as it is, they tend to
eschew plot subtleties and character development for
the creation of symbolic realities that serve to undermine absolutes and destroy traditional myths. The end
result is a pervasive impression of nostalgia, isolation,
and metaphysical emptiness in a universe devoid of
order and meaning. Although this assessment of modern life would seem to suggest an attitude bordering
on total despair, it could also represent the kind of
spiritual purification necessary for the regeneration
of hope and human values, a process delineated by the
sequence of events in "The Handsomest Drowned
Man in the World."

In its entirety, *The Incredible and Sad Tale of
Innocent Eréndira and Her Heartless Grandmother*
may prove disappointing to readers enthralled by the
perfect synthesis of realism and fantasy incorporated

into *One Hundred Years of Solitude*. Nevertheless, in spite of its uneven literary quality, García Márquez's most recent collection of short fiction demonstrates once again his unique powers of invention and stylistic virtuosity.

6

Power, Solitude, and Decadence: A Lyrical Portrait

In 1975, eight years after the publication of *One Hundred Years of Solitude*, García Márquez's long-awaited novel, *The Autumn of the Patriarch*, appeared. The plot of this sophisticated, richly textured work consists of a series of episodes encompassing the long life of an aging, unnamed Latin-American dictator (the patriarch), who, at the time of his death, is somewhere between 107 and 232. The patriarch embodies all the classical evils of despotism. Even more significant, however, is his extreme solitude, which becomes increasingly evident with advancing age and emerges as the principal theme. Other important characters include Bendición Alvarado, the patriarch's mother, formerly a bird vendor and prostitute; his double, Patricio Aragonés, whose assassination creates the myth of "the first death"; a beauty queen named Manuela Sánchez, who vanishes during an eclipse of the sun "arranged" for her by the patriarch; General Rodrigo de Aguilar, chief of national security and the patriarch's right-hand man; Leticia Nazareno, an ex-nun and wife of the patriarch; their infant son Emanuel; and José Ignacio Saenz de la Barra, a cultured aristocrat and predatory sadist hired to conduct the search for the assassins of Leticia and Emanuel.

Like García Márquez's other works, *The Autumn of the Patriarch* has a firm grip on modern Latin-

American reality. The exact setting is never stated,
but the occasional allusions to the Caribbean and the
varied terrain of the country dominated by the patriarch bring to mind García Márquez's native Colombia.
The descriptions of political tyranny and gringo imperialism, though obviously exaggerated, could apply
to almost any Spanish-speaking nation of the western
hemisphere. The novel's temporal realm, as indicated
below, is hazy; nevertheless, the fact that the protagonist's life extends into the twentieth century is evidenced by references to a poetry-reading program
presented by Rubén Darío,[1] efforts of American scien-
tists to eliminate a yellow-fever epidemic, landings
by the United States marines, the spectacular appearance of a comet (probably Halley's in 1910), and the
use of automobiles, airplanes, radios, and television.

The patriarch displays pronounced schizophrenic
tendencies that profoundly influence both the plot and
the aesthetics of the novel. Thus, on some occasions
he acts with sadistic cruelty, while on others he sub-
mits masochistically to the will of those around him.
His split personality is illustrated metaphorically by
the appearance of his double, Patricio Aragonés, who
represents both his mirror image and his alter ego.
The unfortunate Patricio Aragonés is obliged to give
up his own identity in order to become exactly like his
tyrannical master, even suffering torture to make his
feet flat and one of his testicles enlarged. He not only
serves as a decoy against all possible assassination
attempts, but also is joined symbiotically with the
patriarch, helping the latter to withstand the imagined
threats to, and cast off the burden of, his fragmented
self (". . . he had clung to Patricio Aragonés as if he
were himself . . . they spent entire afternoons . . .
counting swallows like two decrepit lovers . . . so
apart from the world that he himself [the patriarch]
failed to realize that his fierce struggle to exist twice

[i.e., his struggle to overcome his fear of self-annihilation through self-duplication and the projection of his fragmented self onto another] only nursed the contrary suspicion that he was existing less and less. . . ." [i.e., he was experiencing the terrifying loss of self]. The patriarch's mirror image also indicates his narcissistic involvement with himself and his resultant inability to love others, characteristics that are likewise suggested by his lifelong infantile attachment to his mother. His monstrous testicle, which he carries about in an "orthopedic cart," perhaps represents a metaphoric defense mechanism against castration anxiety. As a sexual organ of reproduction, it could also symbolize his narcissistic self-duplication and thus the decomposition of his ego.[2] The split with his antithetical self is ultimately expressed when the dying Patricio Aragonés gives vent to his long-harbored bitterness, telling the patriarch how much his people loathe him. Soon thereafter, when the patriarch witnesses the desecration of his double's corpse by a rampaging mob, he identifies intimately with it, "feeling on his own flesh the ignominy of the spit and the chamber pots . . . thrown from the balconies." He compensates for his suffering, however, by slaughtering some of his unmasked enemies and torturing the others until they confess what he wants to hear, that they were paid to participate in the demonstration. He breathes a sigh of relief, convinced that "these people love me." But the next day he orders those who confessed under torture thrown to the crocodiles.

In spite of the political implications of the plot and the evidence of the protagonist's sadomasochistic tendencies, *The Autumn of the Patriarch* is not primarily a political or social-protest novel, nor are its psychological elements of paramount importance. Rather it is a lyrical novel, whose plot and character development are subordinate to its formal design and symbolic imagery. The narrative content is conveyed by a wide variety of rhetorical devices intended to reinforce themes, generate mood, and sustain dramatic movement.

The Autumn of the Patriarch contains six unnumbered units, each consisting of a single paragraph. Sentences tend to be extremely long; for example, the last unit is made up of a single sentence covering fifty-three pages. In addition to the rambling style, the novel's most noticeable innovation in García Márquez's fiction is its shifting point of view that ranges from third-person authorial narration to the first-person-singular and first-person-plural perspectives of numerous plot participants or observers, some identified and some not. Thus the work combines a rich variety of narrative techniques, all of which focus on the protagonist (or his immediate world) and, in their totality, project a unified, all-encompassing portrait of the solitude and decadence resulting from excessive power.

The following description of the patriarch's relations with foreign dictators in exile illustrates the most important of these techniques (indicated in brackets) and at the same time demonstrates the stylistic compression and density of the novel. The ex-dictators inevitably carry

. . . clippings from newspapers . . . and photo albums which they showed to him [the patriarch] in their first audience as if they were credentials [omniscient narrator], saying look, general, this is me when I was a lieutenant, this was the day I took power, this was taken on the sixteenth anniversary of my taking office [dialogue] . . . but he [the patriarch] gave them political asylum without paying any more attention to them . . . and with the same scornful attitude he listened to their deceptive remarks [omniscient narrator] that I accept temporarily your noble hospitality until justice calls the usurper to account [dialogue of an ex-dictator], the eternal formula . . . as if the big fools didn't know that in this business he who falls falls [patriarch's interior monologue], and he lodged them all in the presidential mansion, made them play dominoes until he took their last cent [omniscient narrator], and then he led me by the arm to the window facing the sea . . . he consoled me with the hope that I could go over there [soliloquy of an ex-dictator], look, there, in that big house [dialogue of the patriarch] that looked like an ocean liner run aground on a reef [soliloquy of an ex-dictator or omniscient narrator] where I have a room for you with lots of light and good meals and . . . a terrace looking out on the sea [dialogue of the patriarch] where he liked to sit on December afternoons [omniscient narrator] not so much for the pleasure of playing dominoes with that bunch of bumpkins [patriarch used as a third-person reflector] but in order to enjoy the petty happiness of not being one of them [omniscient narrator].

The novel's temporal design can best be described as a spiral consisting of six circular configurations— corresponding to the six units—each of which begins with the death of the patriarch, then evokes a chain of episodes from the past, and finally ends with a major event in his life. The unidentified narrative voice initiating each section is a first-person-plural soliloquy, reminiscent of the chorus in a Greek tragedy, that alludes to the conditions surrounding the patriarch's death, i.e., the sight of his corpse, his mythical omnipotence, the decaying physical environment, and the urgent meetings held by leading government officials to determine the nation's future course. These motifs, repeated with variations, generate a rhythmic momentum that carries the narrative thread of each unit to a point in the protagonist's life beyond that of the preceding unit until, at the end of the novel, the plot comes full circle.

The following summary illustrates this spiral structure. The first unit deals primarily with Patricio

Aragonés's fate and ends with the patriarch's evocation of the Spaniards' arrival in the new world. The second unit narrates the details of the patriarch's rise to power, his brief relationship with the beauty queen, Manuela Sánchez, and her mysterious disappearance. In the third, the struggles for power and the ensuing episode of the flood are punctuated by the gruesome death of General Rodrigo de Aguilar. The fourth is mainly concerned with the demise of the patriarch's mother, her canonization, and, in the final lines, the appearance of his future wife, Leticia Nazareno. In the fifth unit the principal events include the patriarch's marriage, the assassination of his wife and child, the introduction of the sadist, Ignacio Saenz de la Barra, and the one-hundredth anniversary celebration of the patriarch's reign. The last unit depicts the patriarch's extreme loneliness, physical decay, and death.

The novel's structural design is reinforced by archetypal patterns and universal tensions reminiscent of biblical and heroic myths. Although the patriarch's origin remains obscure, "scholarly texts" claim that he was conceived "without male cooperation" and that his "messianic destiny" was revealed to his mother in a dream. According to these same sources, a fortune teller once asserted that because he was born without lines in his hands, he was destined to become a king. His subjects believe him to be invulnerable to bullets and gigantic in stature, having allegedly continued to grow until he was one hundred years old. At the age of 150, moreover, he supposedly cut his third set of teeth. He is also reputed to have fathered five thousand children and to be endowed with the magical ability to converse with animals, cure all kinds of illnesses with salt, and predict the future.

In reality, however, the patriarch embodies all the opposite characteristics of the legendary hero. His life represents an ironic inversion of the quest myth, i.e., the traditional narration of the hero's birth (often attributed to a virgin), his exploits in love and war, and his rise to power and mastery of his kingdom.[3] The patriarch's mother was a prostitute who readily admits her ignorance of his father's identity. Unlike the idealized legendary hero, who achieves love and communion through valor and self-sacrifice, the patriarch is a lonely tyrant living in terror of an assassin's bullet. Contrary to the idyllic paradise of myth, his residence is invaded by cobwebs, moths, and buzzards, and its grounds, by lepers, cripples, and blind people. The flood, moreover, instead of performing its mythical cleansing function, serves to bolster the patriarch's waning authority when he commands the waters to recede, restores the city, and is loudly acclaimed by his people. Toward the end of his regime the city is again a mass of ruins and, as explained below, the sea a barren lunar landscape.

The novel's spiral structure conveys an impression of mythical time, i.e., a sense of endless renewal, tending to negate temporal progression, and thus escape from the terrors of history, into a realm of absolute stability. Aesthetically, the end result is a kind of static, timeless continuum in which present and past are joined spatially through the principle of juxtaposition. This principle is perhaps best demonstrated in the final pages of the first unit when the patriarch visits the mansion where the exiled dictators are lodged and listens to the tales of their glorious past. While enjoying the magnificent panoramic view of the Caribbean from the terrace of the mansion, he recalls an historic Friday in October when he awakened to find everybody in the presidential palace wearing red hats. After numerous inquiries he finally ascertained that a group of foreigners dressed like the jack of clubs had come from across the seas, "jabber-

ing" in a different tongue and offering beads and red
hats in exchange for the local merchandise. Confused
and intrigued, the patriarch looked out his window
and saw the battleship abandoned by the United
States marines next to the pier, and "beyond the
battleship, anchored far out at sea, he saw the three
caravels." This amusing allusion to the Spaniards'
arrival in the New World, juxtaposed with an image
of twentieth-century gringo imperialism, suggests that
although specific conditions throughout the course of
history may change, the existence of oppressor and
oppressed, especially in Latin America, remains a
constant factor. The fictitious account of Columbus's
voyage also illustrates how a fabulous historical adventure can become imbedded in the collective unconscious and emerge centuries later transformed into
poetic myth.*

As mentioned above, the patriarch's schizophrenic
tendencies profoundly affect the novel's aesthetic
quality, creating dramatic tension and tonal modu-
lations through the constant interplay of contrasting
symbolic images and leitmotifs. These stylistic devices
convey the protagonist's incessant wavering between
self-assertion, resulting from his overwhelming desire
for love and power, and paranoic withdrawal, submission, and death wish, a reaction to his obsessive
fear of the hostile world. The following detailed discussion of the third section is intended to illustrate
this pendulum-like movement, which can be detected
throughout the book.

The introductory passage alluding to the patriarch's decrepitude and death is immediately offset by
a description of his youth when he would mingle with

---

* Portions of this passage are written in archaic
Spanish, a contrapuntal device that offsets the present
and emphasizes temporal recurrence.

his subjects, calling them all by name and visiting their homes to share their meals. On one occasion he even worked for three hours to repair a woman's sewing machine while a group of officials waited for him outside in the street. He was so powerful that whenever he asked what time it was, the reply would inevitably be, "Any time you wish, general." One night he had a masochistic dream in which he saw himself surrounded by knife-wielding men who proceeded to carve his body into pieces. However, instead of being afraid, he felt relieved, pure, and even smiled at the prospect of imminent death. Upon awakening he reasserted his authority by dismissing the members of the senate and the supreme court, obliging them to take refuge in foreign embassies. From this moment on, his retinue consisted solely of a machete-armed Guajiro Indian, whose image becomes a leitmotif symbolizing the patriarch's omnipotence and solitude.

During this period of his life the patriarch acquired the habit of visiting fortune tellers, one of whom told him she saw an armed man with a green mask posing a threat to his existence. The patriarch soon "identified" the man as one of his closest aides, and two days later the unfortunate one inexplicably "committed suicide." Another fortune teller had the unique ability to predict the death of her clients by gazing into the "unequivocal waters" of a washbasin. When the patriarch caught sight of his lifeless body reflected in the basin and heard the prediction that he would die between the ages of 107 and 125, he strangled the woman. Subsequently, the oft-repeated references to the "unequivocal waters of the basins" convey his narcissistic withdrawal and obsession with death.[4]

The disappearance of Manuela Sánchez, which occurred at the end of the second unit, continues to irritate the patriarch, causing him to evoke an incident from his past when he entered the home of a recently married couple, had the husband chopped to pieces by his Indian bodyguard, and violated the young woman. He then directs his thoughts to General Rodrigo de Aguilar, his "lifelong friend," but even he, the patriarch suspects, is capable of treachery and perhaps already has gained too much influence. Thus, in order to bolster his ego, he recalls his loyal Indian protector whose cry, "Here comes the one in charge," was always answered by throngs of admirers chanting, "Long live the *macho!*" or "Long live the general!"

Soon thereafter, the patriarch has a premonition of impending disaster. His mounting anxiety is manifested metaphorically by the stench of carrion coming from the sea, a flock of buzzards he sees from his window, and the flutelike whistle of his enlarged testicle, an absurd recurring motif representing a barometer of his anxiety. The catastrophe comes in the form of a cyclone accompanied by torrential rains that inundate the city. While surveying the muddy lake covering the streets and houses, the patriarch soothes his feelings of anxiety by concluding that God is really his ally and has sent the flood to make him forget his anguish over the vanished Manuela Sánchez. Then, having caught sight of the cathedral towers rising above the flood waters (probably phallic symbols of sadistic domination), he orders the waters to recede, directs the reconstruction of the city, and once again hears the multitude proclaiming, "Long live the *macho!*" The immediate prospect of addressing "the abyss of the crowd," however, arouses his terror and precipitates his flight to his mother's quarters. There, the image of her wringing a hen's neck "with a certain tenderness" in preparation for the evening meal underscores his renewed masochistic desire for self-annihilation.

The inevitable reaction to this state of mind occurs

when the patriarch receives a visit from a young, idealistic adventurer seeking arms to fight wars throughout the hemisphere for the glory of the fatherland. Instead of responding directly to the youth's extravagant request, the patriarch shows him a glass ball he holds in the palm of his hand, exclaiming, "This is something that one either has or one doesn't have, but only he who has it has it, this is the fatherland." In other words, the patriarch perceives the nation he governs as an object to be held firmly in his grasp, never to be relinquished until his last breath. His tight grip on the glass ball, then, is a metaphor of his greed for power and, consequently, of his solitude.

After the cyclone and the ensuing period of reconstruction, the patriarch finds himself once again in such firm control of his domain that he allows all exiles to return except the men of letters, whom he considers more dangerous than priests or politicians. This period of tranquility is soon interrupted by an absurd episode that poses an additional threat to the patriarch. It seems that the national lottery is rigged every week in his favor by having a child draw from a bag of balls the only one that is ice cold. Because it is feared the youngsters will reveal this ruse, they are imprisoned in a fortress where their number eventually reaches two thousand. As parents grow more and more distressed over their missing children, the patriarch has a grotesque nightmare in which he sees the victims not as "two thousand separate children but as an immense, formless animal . . . impossible to destroy." In desperation he has the young prisoners sent by night to the most remote region of the country, publicly denies the rumor of their confinement, and invites a commission from the Society of Nations to investigate the matter. The members of the commission conduct a thorough search, even looking under Bendición Alvarado's bed, but they find all the jails closed for lack of prisoners and therefore conclude that everything is in order. After their departure, however, the problem of what to do with the children remains. For this reason they are sent from the jungle

to the provinces of perpetual rain where there were no treacherous winds to carry their voices . . . he ordered them to be taken to Andean caves . . . he sent them pearls of quinine and woolen blankets when he learned that they were shivering with fever because they were hidden for days on end in rice paddies with mud up to their necks so that the airplanes of the Red Cross would not find them . . . he sent them showers of candy and ice cream from airplanes loaded with Christmas toys in order to keep them happy until he could think of a magic solution, and thus he put them out of his mind. . . .

Nevertheless, the dilemma of the missing children continues to arouse the patriarch's anxiety, which he attempts to suppress through a sadistic sexual assault on a servant woman gathering eggs. He then retires for the night and dreams he hears a multitude of young voices singing a song about a soldier who went off to war and returned in a velvet-lined coffin. This nightmare precipitates his decision to put an end to the intolerable situation. Before dawn he orders three officers to transport the two thousand prisoners far out to sea and to sink the boat with charges of dynamite. Several days later, when the officers report their mission accomplished, he promotes them, pins medals on their chests, and has them executed "like common criminals because there are orders that can be given but not carried out, goddammit, poor children."

The aftermath of this gruesome episode is an uprising led by General Bonivento Barboza, whose troops occupy the Conde Barracks, causing panic in the palace. In spite of his painfully whistling testicle and his secret desire to abandon the capital for some obscure refuge, the patriarch rejects General Rodrigo de Aguilar's offer to mediate with General Barboza and carefully plots his revenge. A mule cart loaded with six large milk containers is sent from the palace dairy to the Conde Barracks. Though highly suspicious, the rebels finally allow the cart to enter under the condition that the driver will taste the milk. Moments later, as they watch an orderly lift the lid from the first container, "they saw him floating in the ephemeral backwater of a dazzling burst of flames, and they didn't see anything more for centuries and centuries . . . because of the tremendous explosion of the six casks of dynamite."

The peaceful period following the aborted insurrection turns out to be a prelude to the third unit's climax and the novel's most grotesque and macabre episode. During this brief interval the self-confident patriarch makes the mistake of taking fewer security precautions, the result of his negligence being an attempt against his life by a "false leper." He suspects the instigator of the plot to be somebody close to him and spends many sleepless nights pacing up and down "dragging his elephant feet," another leitmotif suggesting his unlimited power. One evening while he is playing dominoes with his "lifelong friend," General Rodrigo de Aguilar, the latter's "thoughtful hand" somehow reveals itself as the long-sought "hand of perfidy." The incident convinces the patriarch that a coup against his regime has been plotted for the following Tuesday, when General Rodrigo de Aguilar is slated to offer the main toast at a banquet honoring the palace guard. That evening the guests drink and chat for several hours while restlessly awaiting General de Aguilar's arrival. As twelve o'clock approaches, the enticing odor of tasty dishes garnished with flowers pervades the hall, heightening the atmosphere

of anticipation. Finally, at the stroke of midnight the
curtains open and

the distinguished General Rodrigo de Aguilar made his
entrance, stretched out on a silver platter decorated with
cauliflower and laurel branches, marinated in spices,
browned in the oven, dressed up in a uniform with five
golden almonds for solemn occasions and decorations for
outstanding valor on his sleeve . . . , fourteen pounds of
medals on his chest and a sprig of parsley in his mouth,
ready to be served to his comrades by the official carvers
. . . and we witnessed without breathing the exquisite
ceremony of carving and serving, and when there was on
each plate an equal portion of minister of defense with
piñon-seed stuffing and fragrant herbs, he [the patriarch]
gave the order to begin, eat heartily, gentlemen.

As evidenced by the previous discussion of the
third unit, *The Autumn of the Patriarch* not only relies
heavily on contrasting symbolic motifs to create narrative progression and define characters and themes,
but also makes frequent use of fantasy, the absurd,
and the grotesque. These aesthetic elements refashion
external reality into a seemingly endless picture gallery mirroring García Márquez's highly subjective
view of the world and thus contributing to the lyrical
quality of the novel.

Though fused with the absurd, two of the most
obvious examples of fantasy derive from the death of
Bendición Alvarado, the patriarch's mother, and from
the theme of gringo imperialism. Immediately after
Bendición Alvarado dies from a horrible disease resembling jungle rot, the foul-smelling sheet on which
she has been lying displays a beautiful painting of
her as a young woman and exudes a penetrating fragrance of flowers. Although the sheet is washed repeatedly, both the painting and the fragrance remain
unaltered. Moreover, when her body is transported
throughout the country so that all the people can pay

their last respects, it becomes rejuvenated and on one occasion she opens her eyes and smiles.[5] The subject of gringo imperialism reaches its climax when the American ambassador, having joined with several European powers to strip the country of everything of value, demands the sea. At first the patriarch refuses to comply. Finally, under the threat of a marine landing, he permits a group of American engineers to pack the water and everything it contains "in numbered pieces" and to ship it to the Arizona desert.

The novel's numerous absurd incidents negate the tenets of reason and convey a lack of meaning and purpose in human existence. The result is an overall impression of chaos, often rendered hilarious by gross exaggeration and the ironic elimination of cause and effect. For example, the palace is in a perpetual state of disorder due to the multitude of humans and animals wandering about, both inside and out. Hens' eggs are found in desk drawers, sharks appear in the reception hall, and the patriarch spends much of his time milking his cows, which appear on his balcony and other unlikely places. During the siesta he usually chooses one of his many concubines "by assault," while "everybody remained petrified with his index finger held to his lips, without breathing, silence, the general is screwing." Years later he makes love to uniformed schoolgirls passing by the palace on their way home. Eventually it is revealed that they are really prostitutes in disguise hired by the authorities to keep him in good spirits.

During his final years the patriarch becomes senile, amusing himself with television soap operas made only for his viewing, always with happy endings. Moreover, in ironic contrast to the terror he inspired previously among his subordinates, he is occasionally described as wandering helplessly about the palace grounds taking orders from laborers unaware of his identity: ". . . stay upstairs, sir, because a scaffolding could fall on top of you, and he stayed there, bewildered by the uproar of the carpenters and the fury of the bricklayers who shouted to get out of the way you old fool . . . and he stepped aside. . . ." And shortly before his death, though still wielding absolute power, he himself reveals a momentary awareness of his absurd senility when he exclaims, "I'm just a puppet painted on the wall of this house filled with ghosts."

Another preposterous incident occurs when the patriarch celebrates one of his major triumphs over his enemies by having free schools constructed in every province to teach the art of sweeping. The enthusiastic students first sweep all the houses, then the streets, and finally the highways, accumulating huge piles of trash that are transported from one province to another in official processions with national flags and large signs saying, "God preserve the purest one who makes sure the nation is kept clean. . . ."

Bendición Alvarado is the source of many of the novel's most amusing absurdities. A completely unpretentious woman, she makes no attempt to hide her humble past as a prostitute and bird vendor, who painted live birds different colors in order to improve her business. Moreover, she feels more at home in the servants' quarters, where she continues to paint birds, while her maids try on her clothes and cavort with soldiers in her more luxurious lodgings. She complains about her son's low salary and the heavy burden they must bear, utterly unaware that he has made her the richest woman in the country by putting much of his property in her name. Eventually, she is moved from the palace to a mansion in the suburbs because of her embarrassing conduct. She wore a little bag of camphor around her neck to protect herself from germs, put a beehive on the music-room terrace, raised birds in some of the public offices, and hung the laundered sheets out to dry over the balcony used by the patriarch for his public addresses. She was also in the habit of saying at state dinners that she wished somebody would overthrow her son's government because she was tired of always living "with the lights turned on" (living in the public eye). One day during an official parade she thrust a basket of empty bottles through the window of the patriarch's limousine, telling him to drop them off at the store when he went by. The last straw, however, was her pronouncement in the presence of the diplomatic corps that if she had known her son was going to be the head of state, she would have sent him to school.

Leticia Nazareno, the ex-nun who eventually becomes the patriarch's wife, provides another major source of hilarious absurdities. Every afternoon from two until four o'clock she teaches her husband to read and write, singing the lessons with him and keeping time with a metronome. He becomes so enchanted with the preposterous, phonetically designed ditties (which lose alliterative quality in translation) that he bursts into song during visits by foreign dignitaries. In this way he even manages to postpone the discussion with the Dutch treasury minister over a debt owed to the Dutch government. Immediately after Leticia gives birth to their child, the infant is given the rank of general. Within a matter of weeks, the nation's most celebrated general appears in a baby carriage presiding over official functions or riding in a parade limousine, "sucking with ecstasy . . . on his mother's nipple." He is also given his father's war medals to play with and is allowed to choose the ones he likes best to wear on his miniature uniform.

Every Wednesday, Leticia and her son, accompanied by a bevy of servants and bodyguards, go to the market, where Leticia seizes anything that happens to strike her fancy, ordering the merchants "to send the bill to the government." Her visits become a veritable scourge for, in addition to her boundless greed, all the produce she touches instantly withers. Soon the macaws in the market are trained to sit high in the trees and screech what everybody thinks and nobody dares to say, "Leticia thief, nun whore." The unfortunate merchants gradually accumulate a suitcaseful of unpaid bills and, unable to obtain satisfaction elsewhere, take them to the palace. There they are received courteously by a high-ranking official and even permitted an audience with the patriarch. However, when the subject of the unpaid bills is broached, he dismisses the matter by telling them to "send the bills to the government."

Like the absurd, the grotesque emerges as a major aesthetic feature of *The Autumn of the Patriarch*, its purpose being to create tension in the reader's mind through the clash between the comic and an incompatible element, usually horror, disgust, or physical abnormality. The reader's reaction to this unresolved incongruity can range from civilized repugnance or embarrassment to barbarous glee over the flouting of taboos, but the response is always emotional and never intellectual. Probably the novel's best examples of the grotesque are General Rodrigo de Aguilar's "execution," the national lottery involving the two thousand children, and the patriarch's pumpkin-sized testicle, which, on at least one occasion, whistles like a coffee pot.

A series of scurrilously grotesque events, some of which are narrated by the patriarch himself, occurs during the chaotic period a few years after his rise to power. It seems that at an anniversary dinner attended by the foreign diplomatic corps, General Adriano Guzmán became thoroughly inebriated. Unbuttoning his fly, he proceeded to urinate on the ambassadors' wives, all the while singing impassively amidst the panic, "I am the slighted lover who waters the roses of your garden. . . ." Also during this time Commandant Narciso López was caught committing a homosexual act—described in graphic detail—with a dragoon of the palace guard. Shortly thereafter, out of shame, he put a stick of dynamite up his rectum and lit the fuse.

After his mother's death, the patriarch has considerable difficulty with the Catholic Church over her canonization, the result of which is the expulsion from the country of all ecclesiastical personnel. While the patriarch is supervising the departure of the priests and nuns, who are stripped naked before they are allowed to leave, he is greatly impressed with one of the novices, a plain, robust girl with full breasts, large buttocks, and flat feet. Unable to forget her physical charms, he traces her to a convent in Jamaica and has her drugged and brought back to him in a glassware crate marked, "Do not drop. This side up." Two years later, after many hilarious bedroom episodes, Leticia Nazareno becomes his mistress and, subsequently, his wife. The wedding ceremony, which takes place when she is seven months pregnant, is one of the most grotesque scenes of the novel. Moments after they have given their vows before the priest

Leticia Nazareno bent over sobbing Father . . . have pity on your humble servant who has taken much pleasure in the disobedience of your holy laws and accepts with resignation this terrible punishment, but at the same time . . . she squatted . . . in the steamy puddle of her own water and brought out from among the tangle of muslin the premature infant. . . .

The assassination of Leticia Nazareno and her son occurs several years later when they are torn to bits in the market by a pack of fierce dogs trained to attack Leticia's silver-fox fur pieces. This frightful scene is narrated by one of the patriarch's aides, whose description includes not only the grotesque mixture of the animal and the human, but also poetic images of striking incongruity.

> . . . they ate them alive, general . . . sixty identical dogs that . . . jumped out from between the vegetable stands and fell on Leticia Nazareno and the child without giving us time to shoot for fear of killing the two of them who, it appeared, were drowning together with the dogs in a hellish whirlpool, we saw only the fleeting glimpses of ephemeral hands stretched out toward us while the rest of the body was disappearing piece by piece, we saw fleeting expressions which were at times terrified, at times pitiful, at times jubilant, until they at last sank into the vortex of the scramble and only Leticia Nazareno's felt hat with violets remained floating before the impassive horror of the vegetable vendors. . . .

The passages involving José Ignacio (Nacho) Saenz de la Barra, the cultured sadist hired to ferret out the murderers of Leticia Nazareno and her son, lend an element of grotesque irony to the novel. The patriarch is awed by the young aristocrat whose French accent, knowledge of seven languages, and impeccable appearance, make him unique among the government officials. Thus he easily gains the patriarch's high esteem and, ironically, at times treats him like a subordinate. Soon after Nacho assumes his duties as chief investigator of Leticia's murder, he sends the patriarch a bag of what appear to be six coconuts, advising him to store it in a filing cabinet. Several days later, an unbearable stench leads to the discovery that the bag contains six heads of the patriarch's most bitter enemies. Eventually 918 heads are delivered, one of which the patriarch unhappily recognizes as having belonged to an aide with whom he had enjoyed playing dominoes. Nevertheless, the arrogant Nacho continues his fiendish police operations. He even designs and manufactures instruments of torture, having been told by the patriarch that everything is permitted except "the application of electric shocks to the testicles of children under five years of age in order to elicit confessions of crimes from their parents." As Nacho's power and influence continue to grow, the patriarch's admiration for him predictably turns to suspicion and fear. Therefore he arranges an insurrection against his criminal investigator and looks on with sadistic amusement when the latter's overbearing self-confidence turns to panic and terror. Nacho's horrible fate (he is beaten to a pulp and hanged from a street light with his genital organs in his mouth) becomes an instrument of irony when the masses extol their leader for ridding the nation of a dangerous enemy.

As indicated above, the novel's lyrical quality is determined in part by its abundance of figurative language. For example, the theme of physical decadence, though evident throughout, is perhaps best set forth by the verbal images describing the atmosphere immediately after the patriarch's death. The city awakens from its lethargy that morning "with the warm and gentle breeze . . . of rotting grandeur." In the palace gardens the rose bushes are snow white with "lunar dust." Turkey buzzards tear the screens of the palace, disturbing with their wings the "stagnant time" inside where the air seems "ancient" and the light "decrepit." And stretched out on the floor is "that senile body gnawed by buzzards and infested with parasites from the depths of the barren seabed."

Leitmotifs illuminate important aspects of the major characters, thus fixing them more firmly in the reader's mind. For example, Bendición Alvarado's favorite pastime of painting birds recalls her humble life before she became a prominent figure. Manuela Sánchez usually carries a rose, bringing to mind her youthful beauty, but the fact that the rose withers and dies parallels her loneliness and foreshadows her disappearance. Leticia Nazareno's sexual appeal to the patriarch is expressed by her odor of a "wild animal," while the silver-fox fur pieces she wears after their marriage symbolize the cunning by which she is able to achieve her ambitions. Nacho's beastly nature is paralleled by his ferocious Doberman pinscher, Lord Köchel, which follows him everywhere, even into the patriarch's office. Occasionally leitmotifs define relationships between characters, as for example in the case of the highly ironic phrase "my lifelong friend," which the patriarch uses to express his "affection" for General Rodrigo de Aguilar.

The most frequent leitmotifs, however, allude to the patriarch and serve primarily to highlight his schizophrenic bid for power and domination, on the one hand, and, on the other, his withdrawal, submission, and obsession with death. His longing to dominate emerges through the repetition of phrases such as "I am the one who's in charge," "Here comes the one in charge!" and "Long live the *macho*!" This same characteristic is also communicated by the golden spur he wears on his left heel, his tight grip on the glass ball he holds in his hand, his enormous feet, and his custom of throwing salt to the infirm in order to elicit their love, gratitude, and acclaim. His solitude, and air of submission find expression through the image of his feminine-appearing hands, often encased in satin gloves, languidly waving a white handkerchief from behind the window of his limousine. His withdrawal and isolation motivated by fear become apparent when, upon retiring, he locks his door with three crossbars, three bolts, and three latches before stretching out on the floor face down, his right arm serving as a pillow. And his obsession with death is accentuated by the "unequivocal waters" of the fortune teller's basin and the terrifying flashes of the lighthouse beacon alternating its beam between the lifeless seascape and his bedroom.

In some cases the motifs are repeated with variation in order to render the illusion of rhythmic movement and reinforce thematic content. The best example of this technique is the image of the patriarch "dragging his elephant-sized feet," at first a sign of his power and animal nature but gradually an indication of fluctuating moods, solitude, and advancing age.[6] Thus in subsequent passages he is seen "dragging his big feet like a lover in hiding" (reflecting his initial unwillingness to marry Leticia Nazareno); "dragging his big, captive-elephant feet" (paralleling his fascination and delight with Rubén Darío's poetry); "dragging his dense, decrepit feet"; "dragging his big senile-elephant feet"; "dragging his big feet like a hopeless victim of insomnia"; and, shortly before his death, "dragging his big feet like a specter as he wandered through the immense, dark mansion."

Other motifs allude to secondary social and psychological themes. For example, the oft-mentioned battleship anchored in the harbor underscores gringo imperialism; the absurd image of rich children being ground up for sausage in the slums conveys the deep division between social classes that exists throughout Latin America; the patriarch's fantastic vision of the spectacular volcano in Martinique alongside "the nightmare of Haiti" highlights extremes typical in this part of the world; and the mechanical toys the patriarch purchases for Manuela Sánchez (the beauty queen) reflect the superficial nature of their relationship.

Additional stylistic devices frequently utilized in *The Autumn of the Patriarch* are paradox and metaphor, their purpose being to foster poetic ambiguity, intensify mood, and, especially in the case of metaphor, to render the abstract more concrete. There are numerous examples. In a moment of anger the patriarch pounds the table with his "rough maiden's hand." The old battleship was "longer and more somber than truth." The patriarch "felt older than God in the semi-darkness of dawn." Leticia Nazareno's unborn child speaks to her of "the tender steel of her insides." The patriarch's power is defined as a "mass of slime without shores," and the precariousness of his fate is conveyed by the "quicksand of his power." During the search for Manuela Sánchez's home in the labyrinthian slums, the patriarch wonders which house is hers in "this uproar of peeling walls." The first time he sees Leticia Nazareno, the patriarch becomes aware of her "large blind breasts," and after her return from Jamaica he views her under the "flourlike light" of the mosquito netting. When he finally makes love to her, he weeps, "stunned by the anxiety of his kidneys and the string of firecrackers in his guts." Subsequently, their midday sexual encounters are referred to as "the shrimp broth of the siesta frolic." As he thinks about how to handle a revolt against his regime, the patriarch "inhaled the murmur of recently born roses" and, upon observing the one-hundredth anniversary of his rise to power, he sees the crowds as a "torrent of slime."

In the final pages of the novel the patriarch is awakened in the middle of the night by the ghostly image of death standing over him. During the ensuing moments, the last of his life, a first-person-plural narrator asserts that the patriarch's incapacity for love has made him a victim of the "solitary vice of power," a vice that gradually took possession of him and compelled him to commit many wrongs "in order to keep the glass ball in his fist until the end of time." He has realized all along, we are told, that he acquired his power and glory through devious means, but the denial of this knowledge has enabled him to live with it and deceive himself with the belief that lying is "more convenient than doubt, more useful than love, and longer lasting than truth." Thus, the unidentified narrator states, the patriarch has been condemned to know only "the reverse side of life," never having felt the sentiments of love or happiness that even his poorest subjects have experienced. The juxtaposition of his hermetic isolation with the spontaneous outpouring of joy triggered by his death sustains to the end the duel of opposites typifying the entire work.

The Autumn of the Patriarch is García Márquez's most experimental novel to date and may well turn out to be the most fascinating for sophisticated readers and students of literature. Its principal theme of solitude emerges from the protagonist's lifelong inability to achieve meaningful communication with his fellow men due to his alternating impulses for sadistic domination and masochistic submission. Indeed, symptoms of his neurosis are even communicated to his intimidated subjects, who enthusiastically profess their affection and admiration for him in public while secretly loathing everything he stands for (". . . we would kiss his footprint in the mud and yearn for his agonizing death."). As suggested in García Márquez's earlier works, the lack of brotherly love and human solidarity leads inevitably to social decay, another important theme.

The major thrust of the novel, however, is not political, social, or psychological, but poetic. García Márquez's intention is to project a highly personal, and at times phantasmagorical, view of Latin-American reality by probing the universal realm of subjective experience and thus to create a more original work of art. The numerous narrative voices would seem to function as the writer's multiple lyrical self, while the lengthy, rambling sentences weave a tightly knit fabric of motifs intended to illuminate momentary states of mind rather than to develop characters in the traditional sense. Because the novel's underlying scheme is determined by the fluctuations of the patriarch's consciousness, the plot appears to be molded by contrapuntal images, a narrative technique that substitutes perception for action and in this way symbolizes experiences. This phenomenological approach to fiction casts serious doubts on the existence of an individual's "true self," suggesting instead that personality is a composite of fleeting emotions and exterior masks.

The work's mytho-poetic atmosphere stems from its spiral design, which dims the horrors of lineal history by creating the impression of cyclical renewal, and from the use of archetypal motifs, which bolster the structural framework with universal underpinnings. Mythical patterns, however, are often altered or ironically reversed by fantasy, hyperbole, and grotesque absurdities, probably to cast doubt on antiquated values and revise stereotyped ways of looking at the world. These distortions of objective reality also provide a constant source of humor and thus, unlike the typical social-protest novel, blur and even poetize the shocking incidents of man's inhumanity to his fellow man.

Because of its heavy reliance on the juxtaposition of verbal images, *The Autumn of the Patriarch* can be described as a fluid montage of illuminated moments. It is in addition a work of remarkable artistic balance and tension due primarily to the patriarch's psychic waverings, but also due to its metaphoric language and its constant interplay between humor and horror and between fantasy and objective reality. The literary texture is enriched, moreover, by a generous sprinkling of leitmotifs that help to identify characters, define

mood, and strengthen compositional unity with familiar landmarks.

The most puzzling and least convincing part of
the novel is its ending. Soon after the image of death
appears hovering over the patriarch, the above-
mentioned first-person-plural soliloquy effects an
abrupt change in the narrative tone. This anonymous
narrator's rather bland statement to the effect that the
patriarch's total alienation has resulted from his lust
for power conveys information the reader has gleaned
by the end of the first unit, thus making it seem re-
dundant and even detrimental from an aesthetic point
of view. Equally perplexing is the narrator's attitude
of resignation and conciliation toward the misdeeds
of the past, an attitude unlike any expressed heretofore
in the book.

. . . the only feasible life was . . . the one we saw from our
standpoint which wasn't yours, general, the standpoint of
the poor . . . of our innumerable years of misfortune and
our fleeting moments of happiness, where love was con-
taminated by germs of death but it was still love, general,
while you yourself were scarcely a hazy vision of pitiful
eyes seen through the dusty curtains of a train window. . . .

This narrative voice could be intended to perform
a function similar to that of the chorus in Greek tragedy, i.e., it could represent a final commentary by the
citizenry, whose suppressed hatred and rage have been
replaced by their forbearance, understanding, and pity,
thus indicating the regeneration of love and human
solidarity. If this is indeed García Márquez's intention,
it would appear that he is attempting to portray his
protagonist as a tragic figure, whose suffering and
death have had a purifying effect on his nation's collective psyche. Personally, I find this view of the
patriarch difficult to accept, for in spite of his filial
devotion and agonizing solitude—his only redeeming

features—he remains a monstrous specimen of the
human race, unworthy of the admiration or compassion
usually associated with tragic characters. In my opinion, the novel would have been strengthened both
thematically and aesthetically had the tension between
poetry and horror been maintained to the end, omitting
the first-person-plural soliloquy in the final passage and
leaving any possible sympathy on the part of the reader
to be gleaned from the scenic action or the patriarch's
interior monologues. In this way the cathartic effect
of his demise—if such an effect is intended—would
be dramatically conveyed instead of tritely stated.

The book's ending is not its only flaw. Its impact
would probably be heightened and its artistic value
enhanced were it shortened by at least twenty-five
pages, half of which could be extracted from the relatively tedious sixth unit. Because of the extremely long
sentences and numerous repetitions, those unac-
customed to the stylistic patterns of the lyrical novel
may find this one easy to lay aside. Nevertheless, its
drawbacks notwithstanding, *The Autumn of the Patriarch* in some respects looms as García Márquez's most
memorable literary creation. The work of an astonishing sensibility and prodigious imagination, it tells an
outrageous chapter of Latin-American and universal
reality, all the while maintaining a remarkable equi-
librium between lyrical and narrative art. This jungle
view of Latin-American politics, poetically appre-
hended and recreated symbolically, is only too real
in the world of the 1970s. García Márquez's brilliantly
stylized portrait of a mythical tyrant playing God but
hopelessly trapped in the "darkness of power" is likely
to stretch his readers' imagination to the limit. It is
not only the most original Latin-American novel to
date on the timely subject of political tyranny, but also
an ingenious experiment in prose fiction.

Conclusions

García Márquez's approach to fiction indicates that he has come full circle in at least one respect, namely, in his depiction of subjective states of mind reminiscent of surrealism. Thus, whereas his early short stories are characterized by hermetic morbidity and fantasy, his most recent novel is the most lyrically conceived to date. During the intervening years he has sharpened his literary tools and emerged as a mature, consummate craftsman, the result of extensive reading and experimentation with a wide variety of styles and techniques. The vision of Macondo set forth in *Leaf Storm* reveals possible influences of William Faulkner and Virginia Woolf; Hemingway's aesthetic ideals are brought to mind by "Tuesday Siesta," "One of These Days," and *No One Writes to the Colonel*; other fine pieces such as "Baltazar's Marvelous Afternoon" and "Big Mama's Funeral" point the way toward the perfect synthesis of realism and fantasy displayed in the internationally acclaimed masterpiece, *One Hundred Years of Solitude*; and the most recent works depict a world in which lyricism and fantasy predominate.

García Márquez's fictional universe consists of three major settings: "the town," Macondo, and a seaside village, or, in the case of *The Autumn of the Patriarch*, a large seaport. Although solitude emerges as his most important theme, "the town" is also the

157

scene of *la violencia*. The other two settings provide
the backdrop for the recurring cycle of birth, boom,
decay, and death. Time plays an important role in
García Márquez's works, the horrors of lineal history
serving to convey the failure of man's political, social,
and religious institutions. On the other hand, the repetitive patterns and rhythmic momentum generated
by mythical time create a mytho-poetic atmosphere
that blurs sordid reality and thrusts the reader into a
kind of temporal void where the laws of cause and
effect tend to become meaningless.

García Márquez displays his mastery of irony and
wry humor in *No One Writes to the Colonel*, the pro-
taganist of which emerges as an absurd hero struggling
against impossible odds. The subsequent works reveal
a trend toward a more Rabelaisian type of humor, with
greater emphasis on the absurdities of human existence. These attacks on the tenets of reason are more
than likely intended to unveil the other side of reality
and in this way question the outmoded conventions
that have spawned the disasters of the twentieth century. An antirational outlook on the world is also expressed stylistically through the inordinately long,
rambling sentences and jarring shifts in the point of
view in "The Last Voyage of the Ghost Ship" and
"Blancamán the Good, Vendor of Miracles." In addition "The Last Voyage of the Ghost Ship" presents a
schizophrenic view of reality, depending primarily on
contrasting images to reflect the protagonist's extreme
alienation. The culmination of these tendencies is
reached in *The Autumn of the Patriarch*, García Márquez's best portrayal of solitude and most lyrical novel
to date.

The fact that many of García Márquez's characters reappear under different circumstances in subsequent works creates the impression that his stories and
shorter novels are fragments of a more complete fic-

tional universe. For example, Rebeca Buendía is first introduced in "Tuesday Siesta" as the widow who shoots the youth she believes is trying to break into her house. She is next seen as a rather eccentric character in "One Day After Saturday." Finally, in *One Hundred Years of Solitude* her entire life unfolds as an integral part of the Genesis-to-Apocalypse chronicle of Macondo. The colonels in *Leaf Storm* and *No One Writes to the Colonel* resemble each other in many respects, leading one to suspect that the protagonist of the second book is an extension of the portrait begun in the first. The mayor's brief appearance in *No One Writes to the Colonel* is a prelude to his major role in *The Evil Hour.* And the ineffectual Father Angel plays minor roles in *Leaf Storm* and *No One Writes to the Colonel* but emerges as one of the leading figures in *The Evil Hour.*

The widow Montiel appears as the protagonist of the short story bearing her name, at the end of which she has a mysterious dream about Big Mama. Her connection with Big Mama is clarified in *The Evil Hour* by the fact that she and her husband acquired Big Mama's mansion after the matriarch's death. This relationship between the Montiels and Big Mama constitutes one of the rare discrepancies in García Márquez's works. Big Mama reigned in Macondo, where, we are told, her mansion was dismantled by her heirs moments after her funeral; the Montiels are prominent citizens of "the town."

García Márquez's fiction is also characterized by recurring episodes, details of which are altered in order to avoid monotonous repetition. For example, the extraction of the mayor's abscessed tooth by his enemy, the dentist, occurs in both *The Evil Hour* and "One of These Days." In the novel the episode represents a dramatic climax led up to by the mayor's vain efforts to alleviate his unbearable pain and his forced entry into the dentist's office at midnight with his armed guards. In the short story, however, the mayor arrives alone at eight o'clock in the morning threatening to shoot the dentist if he refuses to pull the tooth. Here dramatic tension is generated by the understated tone and the dearth of details, a technique intended to make the reader exercise his imagination. These successful, though widely differing, treatments of the same incident demonstrate García Márquez's skill as a practitioner of both genres of prose fiction.

Solitude resulting from power emerges as one of García Márquez's major themes, culminating with his portrait of the protagonist of *The Autumn of the Patriarch*. This unforgettable character, however, has at least two predecessors representing important stages in the evolution of the theme: the mayor of *The Evil Hour* and Colonel Aureliano Buendía of *One Hundred Years of Solitude*. The mayor stands out as a realistically delineated, though somewhat enigmatic figure, whose agonizing toothache underscores his separation from "the town" he is sent to subdue during *la violencia*. Colonel Aureliano Buendía initiates his military career determined to overthrow the corrupt conservative government and replace it with a just liberal regime. When he retires to the family home in Macondo many years later, he has become a complete cynic due to the futility of his efforts. His final years spent manufacturing gold fishes reflect his solitude as well as the absurdity of his struggles. Unlike the mayor or Colonel Aureliano Buendía, whose solitude can be traced to their roles in civil wars readily identifiable in Colombian history, the patriarch is a schizophrenic personality whose death obsession and greed for power constitute the basis not only for his isolation from other human beings but also for the novel's plot and formal design.

Although García Márquez's male characters have

no monopoly on irrational conduct, his female characters are usually stronger, more down to earth, and less
likely to be carried away by their emotions, whims, or
abstract ideals. Indeed, in several of García Márquez's
works the contrast between his male and female characters provides an important source of dramatic tension and irony. The most obvious case in point is José
Arcadio Buendía and his wife Ursula of *One Hundred
Years of Solitude*, the former emerging as a rudderless
dreamer and the latter as the mainstay, who, in spite
of her husband's harebrained schemes, manages to
hold the clan together for many generations. Similar
contrasts between husband-and-wife figures exist in
Leaf Storm, No One Writes to the Colonel, "There
Are No Thieves in This Town," "Baltazar's Marvelous
Afternoon," and "The Sea of Lost Time." And even in
The Autumn of the Patriarch, Bendición Alvarado
stands out as a pillar of strength for her wavering son,
the patriarch, to lean on.

The reader of García Márquez's entire *oeuvre*
may be left with the overall impression that today's
world is doomed either to imminent annihilation or
to entropic stagnation and decay. The fundamental
reason for this pessimistic assessment would seem to be
man's lost capacity for love, a defect underscored by
his overwhelming greed for power and material gain.
Nevertheless, ample evidence of eternal virtues is provided by such characters as the impoverished woman
in "Tuesday Siesta," whose strength and dignity dominate every episode of the story; the courageous and
idealistic colonels in *Leaf Storm* and *No One Writes
to the Colonel*; Ursula, the archetype of feminine
wisdom and stability in *One Hundred Years of Solitude*; her husband José Arcadio Buendía, who, though
flighty and irrational, embodies man's heroic quest for
progress and truth in a fathomless universe; their great-
grandson Aureliano Segundo and his mistress Petra

Cotes, whose sincere love makes them charitable toward others; Esteban, the messenger of hope, beauty, and human solidarity in "The Handsomest Drowned Man in the World"; and the generous protagonist of "Baltazar's Marvelous Afternoon," whose creative genius and private world of fabulous dreams represent the antithesis of despair and nihilistic destruction.

As best exemplified by *One Hundred Years of Solitude*, García Márquez's ingenious mixture of realism and fantasy has resulted in the creation of a total fictional universe in which the commonplace takes on an aura of magic and the impossible is made believable. His penetrating insights into the ambiguities of human nature are enhanced by a rich vein of anecdotes and leitmotifs he taps from his private mythology. Though he clearly implies moral indignation against brutality, exploitation, and degradation, he delights his readers with his deft fusion of tragedy and comedy and with his seductive powers of language. García Márquez is presently Latin America's most widely known living novelist. He is, in addition, one of the truly outstanding literary artists of our time. In its totality his work imparts not only the stark reality of an emerging strife-torn continent but, also, through the humanistic and universalizing elements of myth, imagination, and aesthetic perception, a highly original vision of man and his world.

Notes

INTRODUCTION

1. Mario Vargas Llosa, "García Márquez: From Aracataca to Macondo," *70 Review* (Center for Inter-American Relations, 1971), p. 129.
2. Wolfgang A. Luchting, "Gabriel García Márquez: The Boom and the Whimper," *Books Abroad*, Winter 1970, p. 27.
3. Ibid.
4. Luis Harss and Barbara Dohmann, *Into the Mainstream*, p. 319.
5. García Márquez's outstanding talent as a newspaper reporter is also evinced by a volume entitled *When I Was Happy and Undocumented* (1973), which contains twelve human-interest stories he wrote for the Venezuelan journal *Momento* between 1957 and 1959.
6. An example of García Márquez's statements on the Allende regime is his moving article, "The Death of Salvador Allende," *Harper's Magazine*, March 1974, pp. 46-53.
7. "Gabriel García Márquez: De la ficción a la política," *Visión*, 30 January 1975, p. 27.
8. Mario Vargas Llosa, *García Márquez: Historia de un deicidio*, p. 81.
9. Rita Guibert, *Seven Voices*, p. 319.
10. Miguel Fernández-Braso, *Gabriel García Márquez (una conversación infinita)*, p. 65.

1. EARLY GROPINGS AND SUCCESS

1. Luis Harss and Barbara Dohmann, *Into the Mainstream*, p. 314.
2. Mario Vargas Llosa, *García Márquez: Historia de un deicidio*, p. 93.
3. Rita Guibert, *Seven Voices*, p. 326.

2. THE THREAT OF "LA VIOLENCIA"

1. The colonel does not express his acute metaphysical anguish as do many absurd heroes of French existentialism, perhaps because García Márquez, like so many contemporary novelists, makes no effort to define the absurd but instead merely depicts its effects. The negative portrait of the priest in *No One Writes to the Colonel* implies a rejection of traditional religion. Moreover, the depressing allusions to poverty, illness, and death combined with the colonel's final expression of revolt against his sordid reality could be viewed as a revolt against God. As Albert Camus has written, "In absurd terms . . . revolt against men is also directed against God: great revolutions are always metaphysical." (*The Myth of Sisyphus*, New York, 1955, p. 94.)
2. For a more detailed discussion of this idea, see Wolfgang A. Luchting's article, "Lampooning Literature: *La mala hora*," *Books Abroad*, Summer 1973, pp. 471-78.

3. *BIG MAMA'S FUNERAL:* FROM REALISM TO FANTASY

1. For a more complete discussion of mythical allusions in this story, see "Los fundamentos cosmológicos del lenguaje en el cuento 'Un día después del sábado,'" by Raimundo Fernández Bonilla and Magali Fernández

Bonilla, *Nueva Narrativa Hispanoamericana*, January-
September 1974, pp. 17-68.
2. See Judith Goetzinger's "The Emergence of a Folk
    Myth in 'Los funerales de la Mamá Grande,'" *Revista
    de Estudios Hispánicos*, May 1972, pp. 237–48, for
    a more detailed analysis of this idea.

4. MYTH AND REALITY:
THE PERFECT SYNTHESIS

1. Vargas Llosa states that the colonels in García Már-
    quez's books are patterned either after his grandfather
    or General Rafael Uribe, about whom his grand-
    father spoke at great length. (Mario Vargas Llosa,
    García Márquez: Historia de un deicidio, p. 28.)
2. The techniques utilized by García Márquez, especially
    in the last three pages of his masterpiece, are fre-
    quently compared to those of Jorge Luis Borges, the
    Argentine writer whose ironic perspective on the na-
    ture of reality mocks the inadequacy of ponderously
    inflated philosophical systems. The dream, the double,
    and the labyrinth are common motifs in Borges's in-
    geniously conceived short fiction.
3. In modern Latin American fiction, the artistic blend
    of reality and fantasy is often referred to as *realismo
    mágico*. *One Hundred Years of Solitude* is one of the
    best examples of magical realism, both for its aesthetic
    values and universal appeal.

    García Márquez has on several occasions referred
    to the fabulous nature of the Latin American con-
    tinent, basing his opinion on, among other things, the
    chronicles of explorers who have described phenomena
    such as a twenty-meter-long anaconda completely
    covered with butterflies, a brook with boiling water,
    and a place where the human voice provoked torrential
    rains. One is also reminded of the wide variety of
    cultures coexisting in Latin America, from the most
    primitive Indian tribes still living in the stone age to
    sophisticated, ultramodern metropolises. It might be

expected, then, that a continent of such sharply contrasting realities would produce an art form of antithetical elements like magical realism.

4. Vargas Llosa, *García Márquez: Historia de un deicidio*, pp. 23-24.

    García Márquez has also stated that in order to create the kind of fictional world in which the line of demarcation separating objective reality and fantasy would disappear he needed "a convincing tone" that would make the most unbelievable occurrences seem true to life without destroying the unity of his plot. (Miguel Fernández-Braso, *Gabriel García Márquez*, p. 86.)

5. Like many Latin American left-wing writers, García Márquez appears to be somewhat torn between literary and political ideals. On the one hand, he has stated that the ideal novel's political and social content should be disturbing to its readers and, on the other, that *One Hundred Years of Solitude* should not be taken seriously. Still, on the rare occasions when his masterpiece has been criticized by leftists for its flights of fantasy and lack of social commitment, he has replied that his novel does indeed come to grips with all phases of reality. Perhaps his clearest ideas on the subject can be summarized as follows: (1) although he favors socialism, he believes that social-protest literature never has brought about and probably never will bring about revolution, and (2) the revolutionary writer should concentrate on producing good literature in order to regain the interest of the reading public that has been lost as a result of mediocre fiction documenting social evils.

5. FANTASY PREVAILS

1. One of the seven stories, "The Sea of Lost Time," was written in 1961 and published the following year. Of the others, four were written in 1968, one in 1970, and the title story in 1972. Only three of the seven

were published prior to the appearance of the collection.

2. Primarily a poetic movement, modernism lasted from the 1880s until approximately 1916 when its leader, Nicaraguan poet Rubén Darío, died. It is characterized by its perfection of form, symbolic imagery, and escape from reality.

6. POWER, SOLITUDE AND DECADENCE: A LYRICAL PORTRAIT

1. For information about Rubén Darío, see Note 2, Chapter 5.
2. For a discussion of narcissism and its many implications, see *The Double in Literature*, by Robert Rogers (Detroit: Wayne State University Press, 1970) pp. 18-39.
3. For detailed discussions of the quest myth, see Joseph Campbell, *The Hero With a Thousand Faces*, 1968, and Erich Neumann, *The Origins and History of Consciousness*, 1971, both published by Princeton University Press, Princeton, New Jersey.
4. According to Erich Neumann, Narcissus's fascination with his own image reflected in the pool of water signifies his immature ego's attempt to break the power of the unconscious through self-reflection. He succumbs, however, to catastrophic self-love, and his death by drowning indicates the dissolution of his ego consciousness (*Origins and History of Consciousness*, p. 96).
5. It should be pointed out that some of the claims set forth to justify the canonization of the patriarch's mother were refuted by the ecclesiastical envoys sent from Rome. Nevertheless, this whole lengthy episode emerges as a delightful mélange of fantasy and hoax with generous doses of religious myths and grotesque humor.
6. There is a possibility that the patriarch's huge feet also allude to his infantile attachment to his mother,

which borders on an Oedipus complex. Oedipus means "swollen foot," the foot being a sexual symbol in mythology (Joseph Campbell, *Hero With a Thousand Faces*, p. 79).

7. The prototype of the Latin American dictator is the subject of several fine Spanish and Latin-American novels, the most famous of which is *El Señor Presidente* (1946), by the Guatemalan author, Miguel Angel Asturias, a Nobel prize winner. This surrealistic work depicts the reign of terror during the regime of Guatemalan dictator Manuel Estrada Cabrera (1898-1920) and the psychological effect on his subjects. Other novels of this type include *The Tyrant* (1926), by the Spanish author Ramón del Valle-Inclán; *The Great Burundún-Burundá Has Died* (1952), by the Colombian Jorge Zalamea; *The Men on Horseback* (1967), by David Viñas, and *Of Miracles and Melancholies* (1968), by Manuel Mujica-Lainez, both of Argentina; *Conversation in the Cathedral* (1969), by the Peruvian Mario Vargas Llosa; *Reasons of State* (1974), by Alejo Carpentier of Cuba; and *I, the Supreme* (1974), by the Paraguayan Augusto Roa Bastos.

Some critics have made the mistake of attempting to identify the dictator who might have served as a model for García Márquez's protagonist in *The Autumn of the Patriarch*. This character is more than likely a composite of many despots, both living and dead. In addition to the dictators governing the majority of Latin American countries today, one is reminded of the following well-known historical personages: Juan Manuel de Rosas (1793-1877) of Argentina; José Gaspar Rodríguez de Francia (1766-1840) of Paraguay; Gabriel García Moreno (1821-1875) of Ecuador; Hilarión Daza (1840-1894) of Bolivia; Porfirio Díaz (1830-1915) of Mexico; Juan Vicente Gómez (1857-1935) of Venezuela; Gerardo Machado (1871-1939) of Cuba; and Gustavo Rojas Pinilla (1900-1975) of Colombia.

Bibliography

1. WORKS BY GABRIEL GARCÍA MÁRQUEZ, IN SPANISH

La hojarasca. Bogotá: Ediciones Sipa, 1955.

El coronel no tiene quien le escriba. Medellín, Colombia: Aguirre Editor, 1961.

Los funerales de la Mamá Grande. Xalapa, Mexico: Editorial Universidad Veracruzana, 1962. (Contains: "La siesta del martes," "Un día de éstos," "En este pueblo no hay ladrones," "La prodigiosa tarde de Baltazar," "La viuda de Montiel," "Un día después del sábado," "Rosas artificiales," "Los funerales de la Mamá Grande.")

La mala hora. Madrid: Talleres de Gráficas "Luis Pérez," 1962.

Cien años de soledad. Buenos Aires: Editorial Sudamericana, 1967.

Isabel viendo llover en Macondo. Buenos Aires: Editorial Estuario, 1967.

La novela en América Latina: Diálogo (with Mario Vargas Llosa). Lima: Carlos Milla Batres, 1968.

Relato de un náufrago. Barcelona: Tusquets Editor, 1970.

La increíble y triste historia de la cándida Eréndira y de su abuela desalmada. Barcelona: Barral Editores, 1972. (Contains: "Un señor muy viejo con unas alas enormes," "El mar del tiempo perdido," "El ahogado más hermoso del mundo," "Muerte constante más allá del amor," "El último viaje del buque fantasma,"

169

"Blancamán el bueno vendedor de milagros," "La increíble y triste historia de la cándida Eréndira y de su abuela desalmada.")

El negro que hizo esperar a los ángeles. Montevideo: Ediciones Alfil, 1972. (Contains: "Nabo, el negro que hizo esperar a los ángeles," "Alguien desordena estas rosas," "La mujer que llegaba a las seis," "Ojos de perro azul," "Diálogo del espejo," "Amargura para tres sonámbulos," "Eva está dentro de su gato," "La otra costilla de la muerte," "La tercera resignación.")

Ojos de perro azul. Rosario, Argentina: Equiseditorial, 1972. (Contains: "La tercera resignación," "La otra costilla de la muerte," "Eva está dentro de su gato," "Amargura para tres sonámbulos," "Diálogo del espejo," "Ojos de perro azul," "La mujer que llegaba a las seis," "Nabo, el negro que hizo esperar a los ángeles," "Alguien desordena estas rosas," "La noche de los alcaravanes," "Monólogo de Isabel viendo llover en Macondo.")

Cuando era feliz e indocumentado. Caracas: Ediciones El Ojo del Camello, 1973.

El otoño del patriarca. Barcelona: Plaza & Janés Editores, 1975.

Todos los cuentos de Gabriel García Márquez (1947-1972). Barcelona: Plaza & Janés Editores, 1975.

2. WORKS BY GABRIEL GARCÍA MÁRQUEZ, TRANSLATED INTO ENGLISH

"Baltazar's Marvelous Afternoon." Tr. J. S. Bernstein. *Atlantic Monthly,* 221, May 1968, pp. 52-55.

No One Writes to the Colonel and Other Stories. Tr. J. S. Bernstein. New York: Harper & Row, 1968. (Contains: "No One Writes to the Colonel," "Tuesday Siesta," "One of These Days," "There Are No Thieves in This Town," "Baltazar's Marvelous Afternoon," "Montiel's Widow," "One Day After Saturday," "Artificial Roses," "Big Mama's Funeral.")

One Hundred Years of Solitude. Tr. Gregory Rabassa. New York: Harper & Row, 1970.

"Blancamán the Good, Vendor of Miracles." Tr. Gregory Rabassa. *Esquire,* 77, January 1972, pp. 134-35.

Leaf Storm, and Other Stories. Tr. Gregory Rabassa. New York: Harper & Row, 1972. (Contains: "Leaf Storm," "The Handsomest Drowned Man in the World," "A Very Old Man With Enormous Wings," "Blancamán the Good, Vendor of Miracles," "The Last Voyage of the Ghost Ship," "Monologue of Isabel Watching It Rain in Macondo," "Nabo.")

"Death Constant Beyond Love." Tr. Gregory Rabassa. *Atlantic Monthly,* 232, July 1973, pp. 77-80.

"The Incredible and Sad Tale of Innocent Eréndira and Her Heartless Grandmother." Tr. Gregory Rabassa. *Esquire,* 79, June 1973, pp. 125-29.

"The Sea of Lost Time." Tr. Gregory Rabassa. *New Yorker,* 50, June 3, 1974, pp. 32-40.

The Autumn of the Patriarch. Tr. Gregory Rabassa. New York: Harper & Row (in preparation).

3.   WORKS ABOUT GABRIEL GARCÍA MÁRQUEZ

Arenas, Reinaldo. "In the Town of Mirages." *70 Review* (Center for Inter-American Relations, 1971), pp. 101-108.

Carballo, Emmanuel. "Gabriel García Márquez: un gran novelista latinoamericano." *Revista de la Universidad de México* 3 (1967): 10-16.

Ciplijauskaité, Birute. "Foreshadowing as Technique and Theme in *One Hundred Years of Solitude.*" *Books Abroad* 47,3 (1973): 479-84.

Dauster, Frank. "The Short Stories of García Márquez." *Books Abroad* 47,3 (1973): 466-70.

Durán, Armando. "Conversation With Gabriel García Márquez." *70 Review* (Center for Inter-American Relations, 1971), pp. 109-18.

Fernández-Bonilla, Raimundo and Magali Fernández-Bonilla. "Los fundamentos cosmológicos del lenguaje en el cuento 'Un día después del sábado,' de Gabriel García Márquez." *Nueva Narrativa Hispanoamericana* IV (1974):17-68.

Fernández-Braso, Miguel. *Gabriel García Máquez (una conversación infinita)*. Madrid: Editorial Azur, 1969.

Foster, David William. "García Márquez and Solitude." *Américas* 21 (1969):36-41.

Fuentes, Carlos. "Macondo, Seat of Time." *70 Review* (Center for Inter-American Relations, 1971), pp. 119-21.

Gallagher, D. P. *Modern Latin American Literature*. London, Oxford and New York: Oxford University Press, 1973, pp. 144-63.

Giacoman, Helmy F. (Ed.). *Homenaje a Gabriel García Márquez*. New York: Las Américas, 1972.

√Goetzinger, Judith A. "The Emergence of a Folk Myth in *Los funerales de la Mamá Grande*." *Revista de Estudios Hispánicos* 6,2 (1972): 237-48.

González del Valle, Luis and Vicente Cabrera. *La nueva ficción hispanoamericana a través de M.A. Asturias y G. García Márquez*. New York: Eliseo Torres & Sons, 1972.

Guibert, Rita. "Gabriel García Márquez." In *Seven Voices*. New York: Alfred A. Knopf, 1973, pp. 305-37.

Harss, Luis and Barbara Dohmann. "Gabriel García Márquez, or the Lost Chord." In *Into the Mainstream*. New York: Harper & Row, 1967, pp. 310-41.

Kazin, Alfred. "Leaf Storm and Other Stories." *New York Times Book Review*, 20 February 1972, pp. 11-14.

Kennedy, William. "The Yellow Trolley Car in Barcelona and Other Visions." *Atlantic Monthly* 231,1(1973): 50-59.

Kiely, Robert. "One Hundred Years of Solitude." *New York Times Book Review*, 8 March 1970, p. 5.

Leonard, John. "Myth is Alive in Latin America." *New York Times*, 3 March 1970, p. 43.

Lerner, Isaías. "A propósito de *Cien años de soledad*." *Cuadernos Americanos* 1,CLXII (1969):186-200.

Levine, Susan Jill. "*One Hundred Years of Solitude* and *Pedro Páramo*: A Parallel." *Books Abroad* 47,3(1973): 490-95.

Loveluck, Juan. "Gabriel García Márquez, narrador colombiano." *Duquesne Hispanic Review* 3(1967):135-54.

Luchting, Wolfgang A. "Gabriel García Márquez: The Boom and the Whimper." *Books Abroad* 44,1(1970): 26-30.

——————. "Lampooning Literature: *La mala hora.*" *Books Abroad* 47,3(1973):471-78.

Ludmer, Josefina. *Cien años de soledad: una interpretación.* Buenos Aires: Editorial Tiempo Contemporáneo, 1972.

Maturo, Graciela. *Claves simbólicas de García Márquez.* Buenos Aires: Ediciones García Cambeiro, 1972.

Mead, Robert G., Jr. "No One Writes to the Colonel and Other Stories." *Saturday Review*, 21 December 1968, p. 26.

——————. "One Hundred Years of Solitude." *Saturday Review*, 7 March 1970, pp. 34-35.

Menton, Seymour. "Respirando el verano, fuente colombiano de *Cien años de soledad.*" *Revista Iberoamericana* 91(1975):203-17.

Merrel, Floyd. "José Arcadio Buendía's Scientific Paradigms: Man in Search of Himself." *Latin American Literary Review* II,4(1974):59-70.

Mora-Cruz, Gabriela. "Cien años de soledad." *Hispania* LI,4 (1968):914-18.

Morello Frosch, Marta. "The Common Wonders of García Márquez's Recent Fiction." *Books Abroad* 47, 3 (1973):496-501.

Müller-Berg, Klaus. "Relato de un náufrago: Gabriel García Márquez's Tale of Shipwreck and Survival at Sea." *Books Abroad* 47,3(1973):460-66.

Oberhelman, Harley D. "García Márquez and the American South." *Chasqui* V,1(1975):29-38.

Peel, Roger M. "The Short Stories of Gabriel García Márquez." *Studies in Short Fiction* 8(1971):159-68.

Porrata, Francisco E. (Ed.) *Explicación de cien años de*

soledad. Sacramento: California State University, 1976.

Rabassa, Gregory. "Beyond Magical Realism: Thoughts on the Art of Gabriel García Márquez." *Books Abroad* 47,3(1973):442-50.

Richardson, Jack. "Master Builder. *One Hundred Years of Solitude* by Gabriel García Márquez." *New York Review of Books,* 26 March 1970, pp. 3-4.

Rodríguez Monegal, Emir. "La hazaña de un escritor." *Visión,* 18 July 1969, pp. 27-31.

————. *"One Hundred Years of Solitude:* The Last Three Pages." *Books Abroad* 47,3(1973):485-89.

————. "A Writer's Feat." *70 Review* (Center for Inter-American Relations, 1971), pp. 122-28.

Rolfe, Doris. "El arte de la concentración expresiva en *El coronel no tiene quien le escriba." Cuadernos Hispanoamericanos* 277-78(1973):337-50.

Shorris, Earl. "Gabriel García Márquez: The Alchemy of History." *Harper's Magazine* 244, February 1972, pp. 98-102.

Silva-Cáceres, Raúl. "The Narrative Intensification in *One Hundred Years of Solitude." 70 Review* (Center for Inter-American Relations, 1971), pp. 143-48.

Teja, Ada María. "El tiempo en *Cien años de soledad." Chasqui* III, 3(1974):26-39.

Tobin, Patricia. "García Márquez and the Subversion of the Line." *Latin American Literary Review* II,4 (1974):39-48.

Vargas Llosa, Mario. "García Márquez: From Aracataca to Macondo." *70 Review* (Center for Inter-American Relations, 1971), pp. 129-42.

————. *García Márquez: Historia de un deicidio.* Caracas: Monte Avila Editores, 1971.

————. "A Morbid Prehistory (The Early Stories)." *Books Abroad* 47,3(1973):451-60.

Wood, M. "Leaf Storm, and Other Stories." *New York Review of Books,* 6 April 1972, pp. 25-28.

Woods, Richard D. "Time and Futility in the Novel *El coronel no tiene quien le escriba." Kentucky Romance Quarterly* 17(1970):287-95.

Index

        Made the Angels
        Wait," 7
Faulkner and, 7
Neumann, Erich, 167 *n.3*,
        4
*No One Writes to the Colo-
        nel*, 4, 21–32, 45,
        46, 157, 158, 159
    cinemagraphic techniques
        in, 30
    comparisons with *The
        Evil Hour*, 45, 46
    historical allusions in, 26
    ironic climax in, 29
    protagonist as absurd
        hero in, 25–28, 163
        n.1 (chap. 2)
    quoted, 23, 24, 25, 26,
        27, 28, 29, 30, 31
    style, structure and narra-
        tive technique in,
        24, 26, 27, 29, 30,
        31, 45, 46
Nostradamus, 101

*Of Miracles and Melan-
        cholies* (Mujica-
        Lainez), 168 *n.7*
"One Day After Saturday,"
        57–59, 65, 66, 159
    quoted, 57
*One Hundred Years of
        Solitude*, 1, 2, 11,
        67–107, 113, 120,
        126, 128, 129, 157,
        159, 160, 161, 162
    American imperialism in,
        97
    as peak of "boom" in

    Latin-American
        novel, 2
    banana boom in, 68, 73,
        75, 84
    Colombian history in, 70–
        73, 75,
    critical acclaim of, 1
    fusion of realism and fan-
        tasy in, 88, 89, 90.
        See also: magical
        realism
    humor, irony and the
        absurd in, 90, 91,
        92, 93, 94, 95, 96,
        97, 99, 104, 105,
        106
    insominia plague in, 74–
        75, 80, 82
    labyrinthian reality in, 83,
        84, 85, 101
    mythical elements in, 67,
        74, 75, 76, 77, 78,
        79, 80, 81, 82, 83,
        84, 86, 92, 98, 106
    principal characters of,
        69–70. *See also:*
        family tree, 71
    quoted, 72, 74, 75, 77,
        78, 79, 81, 82, 83,
        84, 85, 87, 88, 89,
        90, 91, 92, 93, 94,
        95, 96, 97, 98, 99,
        100, 101, 102, 103,
        104, 105
    rains in, the, 69, 75, 76
        79, 84
    solitude in, 69, 80, 81,
        90, 92, 105, 106
    strike in, the, 68, 69, 73,
        97, 105